Land Use Regulation

Land Use Regulation

The Impacts of Alternative Land Use Rights

Martin A. Garrett, Jr.

PRAEGER

New York
Westport, Connecticut
London

Library of Congress Cataloging-in-Publication Data

Garrett, Martin A.
  Land use regulation: the impacts of alternative land use rights
  Martin A. Garrett, Jr.
       p.   cm.
  Bibliography: p.
  Includes index.
  ISBN 0-275-92802-0 (alk. paper)
  ISBN 0-275-92848-9 (pbk: alk. paper)
  1. Land use—Law and legislation—United States. 2. Zoning law—United
States. 3. Land use—United States. 4. Zoning—United States. I. Title.
KF5698.G37 1987
346.7304'5—dc 19
[347.30645]   87-15637 CIP

Copyright 1987 by Martin A. Garrett, Jr.

All rights reserved. No portion of this book may be reproduced, by any process or technique, without the express written consent of the publisher.
Library of Congress Catalog Card Number: 87-15637
ISBN: 0-275-92802-0
0-275-92848-9 (pbk)
First published in 1987
Praeger Publishers, One Madison Avenue, New York, NY 10010
A division of Greenwood Press, Inc.
Printed in the United States of America

The paper used in this book complies with the
Permanent Paper Standard issued by the National
Information Standards Organization (Z39.48-1984).
10 9 8 7 6 5 4 3 2 1

To Sue

Contents

List of figures		ix
Preface		xi
Introduction		xv
1.	An Overview of Land Use Regulation and Land Use Reform	1
2.	The Administration and Implementation of Land Use Regulation	23
3.	A Model for Optimal Land Use	37
4.	Alternative Forms of Land Use	61

5. Major Land Use Issues and Finalizing a Model for
   Land Use   99
6. Regulating Land Use   125

References   135
Cases   141
Index   143
About the Author   147

List of Figures

1.	Land Use and Negative Spillovers	40
2.	The Entitlements Diagram to Suburban Land Use	89
3.	Wealth, Preference, and Monopoly Effects	91
4.	Zoning Entitlements and Takings	93

Preface

The purpose of this book is twofold. Since the early 1960s land use issues have become increasingly important in American society. Consequently, I began to incorporate land use issues into a typical economics course in urban analysis. It became immediately apparent, however, that there was no one volume or even a group of selected readings that was appropriate for an undergraduate course. The absence of a work involving a comprehensive analysis of land use is probably attributable to the interdisciplinary nature of the issues. An analysis of land use involves an understanding of economic concepts, while the implementation of land use policies occurs through the political process that is guided by the judiciary. An analysis of land use therefore must incorporate economics, public policy, and court rulings.

There is a large body of literature that has been provided by land use professionals, whose background may be law, architecture, geography, and perhaps political science or sociology. It became apparent to me, however, that the best analytical studies have been developed by economists and those in the legal profession. Yet lawyers only occasionally incorporate economic analysis and economists rarely include the institutional structures that experts in land use know are important. A major purpose of this work is, therefore, to provide an analytical interdisciplinary approach to land use issues.

There is, however, an additional purpose behind this work. During the past 12 years I have been a member of a planning commission in a community not unlike many of the communities that have been involved in landmark land use court rulings. Primarily these have been suburban communities that have recently been in the path of urban growth or communities that have experienced rapid growth pressure. From the exposure to the problems that rapid growth imposes on a local governing body and the conflicts that arise between local citizens, the governing body, and landlord-developers, I became convinced that optimal land use can be obtained only through a combination of the free market and regulation.

As an economist and a student of land use I immediately encountered a dilemma. The dilemma occurred primarily because land use regulation, especially zoning, has been harshly criticized by eminent economists and lawyers over the past two decades. Actually, it is probably fair to say that recently there has been a clamor among eminent scholars for a free market approach to land use. This work departs from recent contributions to land use policy in two important ways. If we are to develop an optimal land use policy, we must understand how the existing institutional system evolved, recognizing that change will come only from the existing structure. We simply do not have the luxury of starting afresh. More importantly, it is demonstrated that there is a theoretical economic rationale for land use regulation that, when combined with an administrative law approach, leads to a model that approaches optimal land use.

It will become apparent that this book draws heavily on the work of many scholars in land use. It will also become apparent that there are many areas in which the critics of regulation and their alternative approaches are consistent with a combination of regulation and the free market. In effect, this work attempts to provide a balanced approach to land use policy.

Several people have contributed in various ways to my writing this book. Jack Edwards and David Finifter have made immeasurable contributions. Jack's critique of the first three chapters significantly improved the clarity and organization of current land use practices and court rulings. David has commented on several portions of the work, and through hours of conversation has added substantively to the finished product. In addition, I cannot measure my appreciation for his support and encouragement. Karen Dolan's turnaround time of the drafts, including editorial changes, I also consider a major contribution. On various occasions Sam Baker and Bob Barry have provided insightful comments to portions of the work. And I feel sure Sara Parrott, a former student, enjoyed every red mark she made in editing previous versions of the manuscript.

My debts to others include suggestions from Bob Archibald, Cathy Elliott, John Matthews, and Bruce Roberts. In addition, many students who were exposed to rough drafts provided helpful comments.

There is another group of people who have made immeasurable contributions in an indirect way to this work. I thank John Donaldson who, as a member of the James City County Board of Supervisors, first appointed me to the Planning Commission, and Tom Mahone, in the same capacity, for appointing me to two additional terms. Through the years several members of the James City County Planning Commission, lawyers, developers, and citizens within the community have helped focus my views toward land use policy. I also thank the members of the county administration for sharing their views, especially Jim Oliver, the former County Administrator, and Tory Gussman, the current Planning Director.

Financial support for earlier drafts was provided by the College of William and Mary in the form of a Semester Research Assignment and a Summer Research Grant.

Introduction

An analysis of land use in the United States requires a working knowledge of at least two disciplines: economics and law. It is through the theoretical models developed by economists that we attempt to determine the merits of land allocation in a market economy compared with land regulation, and because the institutional structure of land use has evolved through the judiciary, we must understand the legal rationale that has led to the existing structure of implementing land use. The purpose of this work is to provide an analysis of land use in a market economy, including the rationale that has resulted in the existing structure of land use policy. However, because the existing structure of land use in the United States has recently undergone harsh criticism by both economists and the legal profession, a major purpose of this analysis will be an attempt to put into perspective the existing institutional structure in light of the recent criticisms of land regulation, especially zoning as a form of regulation.

Every society makes choices about how its land will be allocated, and it is important to be aware that these choices reflect society's fundamental values. The prevailing values in the United States have been primarily individual initiative and market determination of land use. Clearly, in the earlier stages of growth when land was plentiful the vision of private ownership prevailed. For example, the federal government followed a policy of disposing of as much public land as possible to private individuals.[1] Planning for growth was nonexistent and what city planning did occur was basically platting streets and blocks in anticipation of urban development. With the open western frontier there was less need to give attention to the adverse impacts of urban growth. When negative impacts of urban development did occur it was thought that the common law of nuisance could provide adequate redress to those who suffered injury.

By the late 1800s the free market approach was beginning to be challenged by urban reformers who asserted that unregulated urban development had detrimental social and economic consequences. Their belief was that public planning and government intervention in the private land use market could remedy these consequences. The early reformers desired a system modeled after those of some European cities that had planned for development, and then zoned or regulated the uses of land to conform to the overall plan.[2] However, the reformers' boldest ideas were not adopted. Instead, the practice of zoning was adopted. As a consequence, communities zoned land parcels for particular uses without the benefit of a plan for growth and development. Until the end of World War II, zoning involved only rather mild restrictions on the rights of private property owners.

In the 15 years immediately following World War II, zoning restrictions primarily involved ordinances confined to subdivision development, with the major land use decisions being determined through the private market. Beginning in the early 1960s a fundamental change began to emerge in views about land use decisions and policy. The change involved an increasing concern over the environment combined with the notion that, from the perspective of local communities, all forms of growth are not desirable. For the first time, many became aware that some forms of development created a local fiscal deficit. Consequently, many local communities began to exercise increasing control over land use. Although communities rarely adopted a no-growth philosophy, the adoption of a controlled or managed growth philosophy emerged in many communities. As a result, a large body of literature during the 1970s and early 1980s has been highly critical of the increased public intervention in land use decisions primarily because it is argued that the increased public intervention has led to exclusionary practices. A major purpose of this work is to analyze the current criticisms within a framework of economic theory and legal theory.

A chronological history of major land use legislation is presented in chapter 1. If we are to develop an optimal land use policy, we must understand how the existing institutional system evolved, recognizing that change will come only from the existing structure. We simply do not have the luxury of starting afresh. A brief analysis of the land use reform movement of the 1960s is also presented in this chapter. Here it is argued that either the movement did have a lasting impact, at least at the local level, or that the American attitude toward the right to private property always included an inherent right that owned property has constitutional protection from negative spillover effects from other property owners.

An understanding of land use policy requires not only some knowledge of the institutional structure, but perhaps just as importantly, an understanding of the implementation of policy. The existing administration and implementation of land use regulation is presented in chapter 2. Although federal, state, and local regulations and ordinances are important, the major focus of this chapter concerns the way in which these regulations are implemented. As will become apparent, it is actually through the process of implementation that a viable method for land use regulation can be achieved.

There is widespread agreement among economists that social intervention in private markets is not warranted unless the markets are not functioning efficiently. It is generally believed, however, that the widespread acceptance of public intervention in the market for land is attributable to the existence of negative spillover effects. Chapter 3 begins with the presentation of a model of optimal land use with and without negative spillovers. This discussion is followed by a summary of empirical studies that attempt to measure the impact of negative spillover effects in urban areas. Although a primary criticism of land use regulation has been that the negative externality argument has been overrated, the empirical evidence is not found to be conclusive.

In chapter 3 a theoretical rationale for land use regulation is also developed. From economic theory two conclusions are derived. First, it has been known for some time that we do not have a theory for the supply of urban land that includes infrastructure implementation and that there are nonpecuniary factors that influence the supply of urban land. Yet this alone cannot wholly justify land regulation in a free market economy. Economic theory does suggest, however, that for optimal land use to obtain in a dynamic setting, a contract must be formed between households and the landlord-developer during two time periods. Land uses must remain flexible through time if optimal land use is to occur, yet contracts must be binding. This inconsistency can be resolved through a jurisprudence system that likes piecemeal changes that are justified through a tradition in American political thinking that legitimizes local decision making by reference to the smallness of local communities, in contradistinction to the largeness of the extended public (the nation). It is through this complementarity of economic theory and judicial theory that optimal land use must include a combination of regulation with the free market.

Although the analysis presented in chapter 3 suggests that land use regulation combined with the free market is optimal from an economic perspective and can be implemented through the existing institutional structure, this is not to imply that the present system is free of imperfections. Within the past decade several alternatives to the existing institutional structure of land use have accompanied the criticisms of the present system. Several of these alternatives are discussed in chapter 4 in order to determine if they may be superior to the conclusions of chapter 3. While it is not argued that any are superior, it is demonstrated that there are several advantages to incorporating some or parts of alternative systems into the existing institutional structure. The alternatives include: Frank Popper's land consumerism movement; Robert Ellickson's covenants, nuisance rules, and fines; Robert Nelson's private neighborhoods; the transfer of development rights; Douglas Kmiec's land use intensity system; inclusionary zoning; and William Fischel's property rights approach.

Chapter 5 incorporates a discussion of several land use issues. The chapter begins with a discussion of land rent followed by a discussion of an issue that only recently have we begun to include in the study of land use, namely, that land use regulation may be a means of social control. The merits of land use regulation combined with the free market are then presented. This section is followed by a discussion of incorporating the merits of suggested alternatives that were presented in chapter 4 into the existing institutional structure in order to enhance land allocation. The discussion then moves to an analysis of one of the most difficult issues to resolve in contemporary land use regulation—the exclusionary argument: a difficulty that stems from the controversy concerning private property rights and collective property rights. A discussion of resource allocation and land use is presented next, followed by a conclusion.

The concluding chapter begins with a discussion of the supply of urban land in order to establish how the characteristics of urban land differ from the characteristics of supply for a commodity. In effect, there is no theoretical supply for urban land. The lack of a supply for urban land combined with the model and the implications of the model for land use in chapter 3 leads to the conclusion that planning is a prerequisite to optimal land use. It is further demonstrated how the conclusions of this work are consistent with those of other commentators, although we reach the same conclusion for very different reasons.

NOTES

1. The following briefly summarizes Jonathan Hughes' (1983: 95–97) analysis of early American public land disposition. By 1853, the land area of the United States was 1.9 billion acres, and as late as the Civil War fully two-thirds was empty and in the public domain. In the actual process of disposal of public land almost nothing went according to plan. The government apparatus was too slow in setting up the system, too cumbersome, and when sufficient land offices were finally established, they were too slow in recording and granting titles. Events moved too quickly. Studies of the General Land Office and its procedures agree that the administration was deficient throughout. Although the sale of public lands was to raise revenues for the government, the federal government actually spent more money disposing of the lands than was received in sales revenues. Considering

what was going on—the wholesale privitization of communal property—the system had one overriding virtue: it was fast.

2. Seymour Toll (1969) provides an excellent historical account of the work, personalities, and philosophies behind the land reform movement that led to the initial adoption of the New York City zoning ordinance in 1916.

Land Use Regulation

1
An Overview of Land Use Regulation and Land Use Reform

An analysis of the extent to which land use is regulated and the impact of regulation on the allocation of land must incorporate an understanding of the evolution of land use controls. If we are to develop policies leading to optimal land use, we must begin with the existing institutional structure, including an understanding of its evolution. Controls on land use are not an innovation of the twentieth century. They existed in various forms in England long before we were a nation. Even the earliest Code of Roman Law, the Twelve Tables, provided for setback lines from boundaries and for distances between trees and boundaries.

Modern fiction has it that property rights have a certain absolutism about them stemming largely from Blackstone's statement that property rights cannot be violated "even for the general good of the whole community" (1966: 139). However, he was speaking of the inherent right of Englishmen to own property—

a fundamental human right in Anglo-American society. In that regard, Blackstone stated that property could be used and enjoined without control or diminution "but according to the law of the land" (138). What the laws of the land will permit in terms of land use controls has broadened over the years, although there have been times of retrenchment as well as extension. Societal and economic conditions often set the trend for a particular era. During periods of slow economic growth, communities often exercise few controls over private-sector development, while an increasing concern over environmental issues combined with economic growth will produce a period of more stringent controls.

Early controls on land use in America extend back into the colonial period, but they dealt with specific problems and were limited in nature. Landowners were not entirely free to use their land in any way they desired prior to zoning. For example, the Massachusetts Bay Colony provided for the assignment of slaughterhouses, tallow chandlers, and other nuisance-like activities to particular areas of Boston, Salem, and Charlestown (Wright and Weber 1978).

Nuisance law and contract agreements such as covenants always presented important constraints. In addition, many cities had adopted limited controls on building bulks and restrictions on the heights of wooden buildings to minimize fire hazards. Courts enforced ordinances that barred specific noxious uses of land from neighborhoods designated for protection, for example, the slaughtering of cattle (1880), laundries (1886), and taverns and liquor stores (1897) (Wright and Weber 1978).

From the outset it must be recognized that planning for the use of land has never been a part of institutional structure in the United States. In America the institutional structure for controlling the use of land is most often divorced from the plan-making system, where such a system exists. This system is unlike that in many European cities where a plan for urban land use is first developed and then implemented through land use controls, where both the plan and the controls have legal sanction. In the United States, land use plans do not have the force of law. Land use controls are derived from the police power that permits the designation of parcels of land for a specific use (zoning).

THE EVOLUTION OF ZONING

The beginning of zoning in the United States resulted from three events within a 10–year span. First, in 1916, New York City passed the first comprehensive zoning ordinance. Second, in 1921, Secretary of Commerce Herbert Hoover convened a committee that promulgated the first version of the Standard State Zoning Enabling Act. Last, in 1926, the Supreme Court sustained the constitutionality of zoning in *Village of Euclid v. Ambler Realty Co.*

The New York City ordinance did not arise from a broad-based need for regulating development throughout the city. Rather, it was designed to address two specific problems. One, the garment industry had begun to develop loft factories above the ground floors of the high-fashion Fifth Avenue commercial district. Local merchants were concerned that garment workers on the streets during lunch hour and leaving work would drive their clientele away. Second, there was concern over traffic congestion and the blockage of air created by proliferating skyscrapers. As a result of these concerns, ordinances were adopted promoting specific land use controls that were to become a classic American formula. Zoning came before planning.

Once zoning was introduced, the idea of districting land uses achieved widespread political appeal. Landowners, especially owners of single-family houses, saw zoning as a means of protecting housing from negative spillover effects created by other forms of land use. There were even advantages from the viewpoint of industrialists, since a manufacturing plant located in an industrial district would be less likely to be enjoined as a nuisance. Between 1915 and 1925, the number of cities with zoning increased to over 500, and by 1930, 35 states had passed zoning enabling legislation. By 1968, over 9,000 local governments exercised zoning powers, including 97 percent of all cities with over 5,000 population. Today, Houston is the only major city without zoning.

The constitutionality of zoning ordinances was initially tested in *Village of Euclid v. Ambler Realty Co.* In 1922, the Village of Euclid, a suburb of Cleveland, adopted an ordinance establishing a comprehensive zoning plan for regulating the location of various types of land uses. Ambler Realty owned a 68–acre tract of land in Euclid that it intended to develop and sell for industrial uses. The zoning ordinance restricted the use of the parcel, and Ambler Realty contended that the restriction would confiscate and destroy a great portion of the value of the land. The decision of the Supreme Court clearly manifested the rationale of the Court. Because zoning placed a new restriction on the use of property for which compensation was not provided, zoning had to derive its legal basis from the police power. The right of a community to determine the uses of certain parcels of land found justification in some aspect of the police power asserted for the public welfare. Actually, the Court stipulated that even apartment houses affect the environment of single-unit family neighborhoods because they come very near to being nuisances.

Some 40 years later the Supreme Court reaffirmed the philosophy that the environment of single-unit family residences was a valid exercise of the police power. In *Village of Belle Terre v. Boraas* (1974), the Court found that the restriction of land use to single-family dwellings to provide an environment where yards are wide, people are few, and motor vehicles are restricted is a legitimate guideline in a land use project addressed to family needs. Here a caveat is necessary. Belle Terre was a village on Long Island of 220 homes with 700 people and an area of less than one square mile. To extend this logic to average-sized communities (political entities) seems rather presumptuous. It is clear, however, that the Court ratified the philosophy of the 1920s that households do have a constitutional right to live in single-unit family neighborhoods.

The rapid adoption of zoning in urban areas throughout the nation reflects a clear manifestation of an underlying distrust in the market in the allocation of land. This distrust stems from the ease with which negative spillovers can arise in a free market for land. While examples abound in any community, Seymour Toll's (1969) illustrative example is well worth repeating. In the 1850s and 1860s, the unquestioned queen and arbiter of New York society was (The) Mrs. William B. Astor. She and her sister-in-law, Mrs. John Jacob Astor III, occupied adjacent mansions on Fifth Avenue, both built in 1859. During this time there ensued a long and incredibly dull intramural contest over whether the wife of William Waldorf Astor or his aunt, Mrs. John Jacob Astor III, would be *The* Mrs. Astor. In Toll's words:

William Waldorf Astor ragefully abandoned the struggle, hurled a judgment that "America was not a fit place to live," and repaired permanently to England. ... Wishing to leave his socially competitive aunt a suitable expression of his regard for her, he committed vendetta by skyscraper, violating her mansion by demolishing his and building the Waldorf Hotel on its site (1969: 93–94).

THE TAKING ISSUE

While zoning became the tool for reducing negative spillovers, its implementation as a means of controlling land use has always had to deal with a fundamental tenet of a capitalistic system - the right to private property. During the same era in which the Supreme Court rendered a decision on zoning, the Court issued a landmark decision involving the "taking issue" in *Pennsylvania Coal Co. v. Mahon* (1922). Because of the crucial importance of this decision in subsequent land use, it is worth examining the background of this case in some detail.

The "taking issue" grows out of the Fifth Amendment of the Constitution: "nor shall private property be taken for public use without just compensation." Thus, if a judicial decision by a government, through whatever means, has so acted as to "take" private property for public use, then the landowner must be compensated. Regulation that completely restricts or substantially impairs the property of a landowner rendering the property "taken" is unconstitutional because compensation has not been paid to the property owner.

The Pennsylvania Coal case involved "surface subsidence" by the mining of coal that removes the earth's support from under the surface. Rich, anthracite coal fields were present in nine counties in northeastern Pennsylvania, including mines under many towns and cities throughout the region. In 1922, the year Pennsylvania Coal was decided, Scranton, the largest city in the region with a population of 137,000, had experienced damages from subsidence that included broken gas mains, streets with humps and sags, broken sewer lines, and collapsed buildings. The Pennsylvania legislature had not been insensitive to the difficulties facing the region. A Governor's Commission report in 1913 resulted in a law that forbade mining under municipalities unless sufficient supports were erected to prevent subsidence, but cave-ins continued. In 1921, an Act of Pennsylvania, commonly known as the Kohler Act, was passed that prohibited the mining of coal that caused subsidence of any building, structure, or transportation system within the limits of a designated class of cities.

The Mahons owned a home and property. The deed included an express provision reserving the mineral rights of their property to the Pennsylvania Coal Company, and a waiver of any claim against the company for subsidence damage. Actually, the property had originally been owned by the coal company and sold 40 years earlier, with the company maintaining the mineral rights. On September 2, 1921, the Mahons received a letter from the Pennsylvania Coal Company with this notification: "You are hereby notified that mining operations beneath your premise will by September 15th have reached a point which will then or shortly thereafter cause subsidence and disturbance to the surface of your lot."[1]

After receiving the letter Mahon sought to have mining operations beneath his property permanently enjoined, alleging that the Kohler Act made any future mining on his property illegal. Mahon admitted the existence of the Coal Company's rights and the Coal Company did not challenge the facts alleged by Mahon. Rather, the Company denied liability on the ground that the Kohler Act was unconstitutional. Pennsylvania Coal alleged that the Kohler Act impaired the obligation of contracts, and it took private property without due compensation.

Upon appeal to the Supreme Court, Mr. Justice Holmes concentrated on the taking claim. The issue was whether the Kohler Act was simply an exercise of the police power to protect the public health, safety, and welfare against the hazard of subsidence or was the act merely a means of taking the coal company's property without paying for it. Holmes concluded that the Kohler Act was a violation of the Fourteenth Amendment due process clause, which incorporated the Fifth Amendment's taking issue. Holmes further stated what would become the test for many future decisions: "The general rule at least is, that while the property may be regulated to a certain extent, if regulation goes too far it will be recognized as taking" (Bosselman, Callies, and Banta 1973: 136).

The use of this vague rule can only be called a test in a very general sense and illustrates how judges can become the ultimate arbiters of what can be done rather than legislators either at the federal or state level. It was within this legal environment that the rapid growth of the 1950s and early 1960s took place. In practice, if not in early zoning theory, one of the purposes of zoning was to protect neighborhoods from uses that threatened to reduce the quality of the neighborhood environment. The role of zoning in protecting neighborhood quality was widely recognized and practiced.

Throughout the rapid growth of the post–World War II era, however, communities rarely adopted land use management policies. Local governments were reluctant to use the courts in issues involving land use and, for the most part, permitted changes in land uses to suit the owners of private property. Perhaps local governments perceived the taking issue as a threat to land use regulations and failed to exercise their powers, or they backed down easily when challenged.

If so, there was a myth to the taking clause—a myth that assumed less land can be regulated than is permitted by the courts. In a survey of court cases throughout this period, Bosselman, Callies, and Banta reach the following conclusion:

> Our strongest impression from this survey is that the fear of the taking issue is stronger than the taking clause itself. It is an American fable or myth that a man can use his land in any way he pleases regardless of his neighbors. The myth survives, indeed thrives, even though unsupported by the pattern of court decisions. Thus, attempts to resolve land use controversies must deal not only with the law, but with the myth as well (1973: 318–319)

Post–World War II land regulation was thus strongly influenced by two factors: a progrowth philosophy that pervaded local jurisdictions throughout the nation and this apparent myth inhibiting land use regulations. This was an era in which an antigrowth outlook was virtually un-American. Growth and development were believed to benefit every community. The logic was simple, persuasive, and widespread. Industrial and commercial growth created both direct and indirect employment and income and thereby benefitted the community at large. In addition, an increase in real estate property values would enable the community to provide more or better public services or lower the local property tax rate. These attitudes toward growth pervaded most communities throughout the 1950s.

The major land use regulations that were implemented during this era primarily applied to neighborhoods. Basically, they were in the form of ordinances that set minimum standards for roads, sewer and water construction, culverts, and setbacks. This is not to imply, however, that planning for growth and development was completely absent. Any decision concerning the location of transportation infrastructure or sewer and water infrastructure, in some sense, reflects planning for growth. Local public officials did make these decisions, yet it was the private market that determined the uses of land as a result of the infrastructure implementation.

THE CHANGING ATTITUDE TOWARD GROWTH AND DEVELOPMENT

A changing public attitude toward growth and development within many local communities emerged in the early 1960s. Two factors were simultaneously responsible for this change. First, there was an increasing concern over environmental issues, and it was apparent that certain types of economic development were detrimental to the environment. Second, economic analysis began to demonstrate that all forms of economic development did not generate a positive fiscal impact in every community. In fact, it could easily be demonstrated that some types of growth generated a local fiscal deficit. Heretofore, economists had been primarily concerned with the positive fiscal impacts, and they had not taken into consideration the negative impacts.

The fiscal impact is easily explainable. Why economists did not investigate the negative impact earlier is inexplicable. It is now widely known that given the per student cost of local public education, the number of children per household enrolled in the public school system, and the average contribution of each household to local revenues, households create a local fiscal deficit for most communities—a deficit that is normally offset by commercial-industrial contributions to local revenues. This deficit obviously presented a fiscal problem for communities when the relative growth in households exceeded the relative growth in the commercial-industrial sector. It even became apparent that certain types of industrial growth could generate a local fiscal deficit. That is, if the local revenues from the industrial growth, including multiplier effects, did not equal the deficit generated by the growth in households resulting from inmigration brought about by the increased employment opportunities, certain types of industrial growth generate a local fiscal deficit. Communities thus began to analyze the fiscal impact of growth and development and preferred to exclude growth that might cause an increase in local taxes in order to maintain the existing level of public services.

The concern over the environment and the preservation of natural resources gained increasing momentum throughout the 1960s, and it was widespread. The right to make money buying and selling land had long been a cherished American folkway. Yet, in an increasingly crowded and polluted environment, many members of society were beginning to question the market mechanism in the allocation of land. They were questioning the right of unrestricted land use regardless of its impact on society.

The changes began with local ordinances regulating land use and in state legislation, which was usually tested through the judiciary. Perhaps the best, early illustration manifested in a court decision can be found in *Candlestick Properties, Inc. v. San Francisco Bay Conservation and Development Commission* (1970). The San Francisco Bay Conservation and Development Commission is a regional agency sanctioned by the California legislature to deal with the ecological problems associated with land use and development in and immediately adjacent to the bay. The commission has strong powers of review over both public and private development within the bay and adjoining wetlands. The legislation proclaimed the public interest in preserving the bay, recognizing the inherent danger in unregulated fill activity. The commission was directed to prepare a comprehensive plan for the conservation of the shoreline and to issue permits for any proposed project that involved fill or dredging of the bay.

Candlestick Properties had purchased a parcel of land that was submerged by high-tide waters of the bay with the purpose of depositing fill from construction projects. Candlestick alleged that the land had no value for any other purpose. The company was denied a fill permit by the commission and sought damages for an alleged taking of its property. In upholding the commission's decision, the California Court of Appeals explained its view of the modern attitude toward the police power. Citing one of its earlier decisions, the court declared:

In short, the police power, as such, is not confined within the narrow circumspection of precedents, resting upon past conditions which do not cover and control present day conditions ... that is to say, as a commonwealth develops politically, economically, and socially, the police power likewise develops, within reason, to meet the changed and changing conditions.[2]

Citing *Pennsylvania Coal v. Mahon,* the court conceded the plaintiff's argument that an undue restriction on the use of private property would be as much a taking as appropriating or destroying it would be. Nevertheless, the court expressly found the *Pennsylvania Coal v. Mahon* case inapplicable to the facts of this case:

It cannot be said that refusing to allow appellant to fill its bay land amounts to an undue restriction on its use. In view of the necessity for controlling the filling of the bay ... it is clear that the restriction imposed does not go beyond proper regulation such that the restriction would be referable to the power of eminent domain rather than the police power.[3]

The Candlestick decision reflected the "new mood" toward land use practices. Throughout the 1970s courts continued to view favorably laws affecting wetlands, shorelands, navigable waterways, endangered species, and conservation. The overall environmental impact of land uses was viewed predominantly by the courts as legitimate regulation under the police power, and they did not constitute taking under eminent domain.

The "new mood" had not, however, reached its peak in judicial decisions. While there was a strong tendency for the courts to approve land use regulations if the purpose of the regulation was statewide or regional, local land use decisions were also supported with a reasonable degree of consistency. Judicial decisions do suggest, however, that the courts require substantial evidence supporting the need for land use regulations and evidence that the regulations will be implemented in a reasonable and equitable manner. In addition, the courts have expressed misgivings about permitting local governments to enforce strict regulations in the absence of a plan that took into consideration a larger area. This philosophy, although limited to certain states, was reflected in two landmark decisions: one involving the town of Ramapo, New York, and the other, Petaluma, California.

The township of Ramapo was faced with a situation parallel to that of many suburban communities during the decade immediately following World War II. Ramapo was a suburban and rural community consisting of roughly 50 square miles of unincorporated land in Rockland County, approximately 25 miles north of midtown Manhattan. The township included several incorporated villages and, under New York law, they exercised exclusive control over land use within their jurisdictions. During the 1960s the township came under severe development pressure because of increased accessibility to New York City resulting from the construction of the New York State Thruway, the Tappan Zee Bridge, and the extension of the Garden State Parkway. The population more than doubled between 1960 and 1970.

In 1965, efforts were initiated to control this rapid growth and, in 1966, the township adopted a master development plan. The plan proposed to hold the population increase to a moderate rate in order to preserve the community's rural, semirural, and suburban character. The development plan was followed by a Comprehensive Zoning Ordinance that designated over 90 percent of the township's area for residential use, with substantial areas zoned for large minimum lot sizes. The only provision for multifamily housing was housing for the elderly, located in buffer zones between single-family and commercial uses. However, the most distinguishing feature of this effort was the adoption of a Capital Budget Program followed by an Amended Zoning Ordinance to insure the timing of the development. The Capital Program specified the location and the sequence in which further capital improvements, such as sewer, water, and roads, were to take place. Capital improvements were to be provided in three separate geographic areas of the township in six-year sequences. At the end of 18 years, the township expected to reach its maximum development capacity, including the provision of all needed public services.

In effect, the ordinance prohibited residential development until adequate supporting facilities were available by requiring a developer to obtain a special-use permit from the town board. A permit was to be issued only if the proposed development earned sufficient development points based on: public sewers or approved substitutes, adequate drainage, improved recreation facilities, public school sites, roads improved with curbs and sidewalks, and firehouses. The right to develop residential areas was thus tied to the presence of municipal improvements and services. The township contended it was not eliminating future growth, only deferring growth until adequate facilities would be made available to accommodate the growth. Because the township did not have the financial resources to provide adequate public services throughout the entire area within a relatively short span of time, control of the location and timing of future development would enable the township to provide the necessary services within reasonable fiscal constraints. Moreover, the developer could ascertain when a particular parcel of land met the criteria for development because the right to develop was tied to a time schedule for the provision of public services, rather than the actual date of provision.

In *Golden v. Planning Board of Town of Ramapo* (1972), the New York Court of Appeals upheld the development timing ordinance, but criticized the enabling legislation for its failure to include a regional element. Experience has shown, said the court, "serious defects" in community autonomy in land use controls. The court stipulated that ordinances such as Ramapo's raise serious questions that cannot be solved by one community alone. Statewide or regional control of planning would ensure that interests broader than those of the municipality underlie various land use policies.

While the Ramapo decision recognized the unconstitutionality of any ordinance aimed at exclusion, the court found that the amendments sought to achieve growth by the efficient use of land through timed and sequential growth. The court believed the town was not attempting to keep out population. Instead, it was attempting to have well-ordered growth in order to prevent deterioration and blight.

In *Construction Industry of Sonoma County v. City of Petaluma* (1976), the California court went even further than the New York court in permitting local control over growth and development. The City of Petaluma, located 45 miles from San Francisco and a part of the San Francisco Bay Area metropolitan region, had grown rapidly during the early 1960s, and population projections indicated continued rapid rates of growth, especially in single-unit family dwellings. Faced with increased pressures for growth, the city council adopted a group of resolutions, known as the "Petaluma Plan." The program required that each year only 500 "development units" could be approved for construction, and a "greenbelt" around the city was established to serve as a boundary for urban expansion for at least five years. A "development unit" was defined as part of a project involving five or more units: thus single-family dwellings not part of a project involving five or more units and apartments of four units not a part of a larger project were not included. A complicated point system, measuring factors such as architectural design, recreational facilities, environmental design, and the availability of low- and moderate-income units, was developed to help determine which projects would be approved.

The purpose of the plan, according to the city, was to promote orderly development, to prevent urban sprawl, and to provide for a variety of building types and densities, including units for low-income and moderate-income families. It is interesting to note, however, that in the preamble to the plan is the intent to protect the small-town character and open spaces and that it "shall be the policy of the City to control its future rate and density of growth" (J. Rose 1974, 180). In upholding the Petaluma Plan, the court relied upon the holdings in *Village of Belle Terre v. Boraas* and *Ybarra v. Town of Los Altos Hills* (1974). In Boraas, the Supreme Court upheld an ordinance requiring that all residences be single-unit family dwellings on the grounds that preservation of quiet neighborhoods serves a legitimate interest under the police power. In Los Altos Hills, an ordinance requiring one-acre minimum lot sizes was upheld on the grounds that it served a legitimate interest in the preservation of a rural environment. In Petaluma, the court reasoned that the plan was less exclusionary than the ordinances upheld in Boraas and Los Altos Hills. Also, the plan served a legitimate government interest within the concept of public welfare because it sought to preserve the small-town character, open spaces, and low-density population, and it sought to promote orderly growth.

The significance of the Ramapo and Petaluma decisions is apparent, yet their impact on national land use regulations must be kept in perspective. In upholding the timing and sequence of growth, the courts have expressed concern over local land use controls. In addition, some courts have indicated a preference for regional and state control, suggesting the courts are concerned that parochial interest in growth and development may not be in the best interest of public welfare. Communities must, therefore, be able to demonstrate that managed growth enhances welfare. More importantly, however, is that many courts have expressed a strong preference for private rights. Courts vary a great deal, especially at the lower level, and many, if not most, state courts would have thrown out the type of restrictions permitted in Petaluma and Ramapo. For example, Pennsylvania and Virginia courts have taken a dim view of much less restrictive rules to promote growth at a normal rate (Siegan 1976: 108).

THE LAND USE REFORM MOVEMENT

There was a land use reform movement in the 1960s, but we might debate how successful it was. As previously mentioned, prior to the 1960s, land use regulations primarily focused on subdivision ordinances adopted by local communities where zoning had been adopted. Many communities, especially rural communities, had no form of regulation prior to the 1960s, and some have yet to adopt land use controls. Hence, land use was determined through the private market with nuisance law being the only restrictive factor to the uses of any parcel of land. Aside from subdivision regulations in urban areas, very little existed in the way of land use regulations at the local level, and there were practically no restrictions at the state level.

If land use reform was to occur, new state agencies had to be established along with local restrictions. But reform was never easy to accomplish, even among those states in the forefront of environmental reform such as California, Florida, and Vermont. The new agencies were needed to regulate active, politically powerful development industries that objected strenuously to state regulation. The opponents of land use reform owned large amounts of land, controlled large numbers of jobs, and were the source of a large part of the state's tax revenues, campaign contributions, public construction, urban development, and general economic growth. They could concentrate their energies and were more adept at publicizing the cost of new land use programs than were reformers at explaining their benefits. The lobbying efforts of these groups in state legislatures far exceeded those of the environmentalists.

In addition, the land use reform movement had to contend with a wide range of characteristically American attitudes, including the private property ethic, the contempt for bureaucracy, and the desire to limit governmental control. The primary opposition to land use controls invariably reduces to the long-held perception that owners feel that their land is theirs to do with as they please, including the right to purchase and sell land for a profit. Moreover, this notion was continually reinforced by the fact that enormous profits had been and can be made in the purchase and sale or purchase-development and sale of land. Quoting from *The Politics of Land-Use Reform,* a Vermont developer explained:

Nine out of ten people speculating in land never really make it big. But the promise that they might hit the jackpot is what keeps them at it. And the biggest defenders of the right to get all you can out of land will not be the one winner, but the nine losers, who can always hope that someday they'll score. Our land use law seems to take away that hope, so of course it has tough sledding. Ninety percent of land use, a Maryland farmer told Robert Healy, is making a buck (Popper 1981: 212).

Many people have invoked landownership as a reason for opposing land use regulation. Such opposition has been voiced not just by farmers of land in the path of urban growth, but also by many small suburban and urban home owners, developers of projects of small, medium, and large sizes, and large corporations that own large portions of land throughout the country. Realtors especially desire minimal regulation because it is easier to sell parcels of land if there are no restrictions as to how the land can be developed. Few restrictions may also lead to greater speculation in land, hence more commissions for realtors.

The uphill battle confronting land use changes was therefore initially accomplished with extreme compromise, sometimes to the extent that it had dubious impact, especially at the state level. Not only was the political influence of landed interest groups effective in state legislatures, but it was also apparent that local communities did not want their governance over land use issues usurped by the state. While there are obvious areas of land control that should be implemented through state and regional agencies, such as pollution of natural resources and water use, with few exceptions to date, state and regional agencies are nonexistent or have little power for implementation of policy. Critics of land use reform, to the extent that it has occurred, have suggested that reformers are simply unaware or refuse to recognize either the emotional or political strength of the American tradition of free-enterprise individualism (Popper 1981: 212).

The same uphill battle was encountered at the local level. However, here the long-run outcome runs counter to the claim that the impact of land reform has been minimal. It is important, therefore, to have an understanding of how land reform, or how the new mood toward land use, was implemented into local land use policy.

The existing institutional structure of land use regulation in the United States, at the local level, permits communities to adopt zoning ordinances. Initially, considerable compromise is necessary if a zoning ordinance is to have support of the electorate. This is especially true in suburban communities, which are part of a metropolitan area but still contain large amounts of undeveloped rural land. Initially, in the rural or agricultural stage of those communities that will eventually fall in the path of urban growth, zoning does not or rarely exists. As the community slowly becomes suburban, it is normally the urban element of the community that initiates the introduction of zoning ordinances. Major compromises must be made. The rural or agricultural sector strongly adheres to the free-enterprise right to private property, preferably with no regulation and at most minimal regulation. The urban element normally desires density controls along with segregation of major land uses with accommodating infrastructure. Thus, compromise is necessary. In order to garner support from the rural populace in the adoption of the initial zoning ordinance, the agricultural zone in the ordinance normally permits many different forms of development, including light commercial and housing development. Similarly, in order to accommodate the desires of the urban element, segregation of land uses and density requirements are incorporated. For example, when zoning is initially enacted, it is not uncommon to find little or no land prezoned for multiunit family housing, while subdivisions are permitted throughout the agricultural sector.

During the 1960s and increasingly throughout the 1970s, most communities, rural and urban, developed comprehensive plans. These plans were normally initially developed by professional planners, presented to the public at public forums, and then altered to take into consideration public input. The comprehensive plan is, in effect, exactly what the name implies. It delineates the existing development of the community and the geographical areas of future growth into major categories, that is, commercial, industrial, and residential, taking into consideration the existing development, existing infrastructure, and future infrastructure. It is, in effect, truly a plan for the development of the community.

The comprehensive plan most often encounters strong opposition from the same constituencies who initially opposed zoning because it stipulates what type of growth is to occur in specific geographic areas of the community, and it often includes the density of development for specific geographic areas. Although the geographic areas may not be so specific as to apply to all parcels of land, landowners have a general notion of what type of growth is designed for their parcel. Many landowners, therefore, have been perhaps more vehemently opposed to the comprehensive plan than to the adoption of the zoning ordinance because the plan offers fewer concessions to landowners than the compromises reached in the adoption of the initial zoning ordinance. Again, major compromises had to be reached. Consequently, in every community there are many discrepancies between the comprehensive plan as it was adopted and the way in which parcels of land have been zoned.

Because the land reform movement of the 1960s was not successful in achieving significant changes in land use controls through state legislatures, there are those who believe that one of the most impressive achievements of the movement was that it survived the 1970s at all (Nelson 1984; Popper 1981). Here is where they have not understood the strength of the movement and the direction it took. While it is true that the comprehensive plan has no statutory power, communities increasingly apply land use regulation in a manner consistent with the plan. With few exceptions, in any request for a zoning change, special use permit, or variance to the existing zoning of a parcel of land, the staff report by the planning agency of the local administration to the zoning commission and the local governing body includes a statement indicating whether the requested change is in conformance with the comprehensive plan. And, while the comprehensive plan is not laid in concrete, the recommendation by the staff is strongly influenced by whether or not the requested change conforms to the existing plan. Moreover, it is not difficult to understand how the land reformers have been able to implement land use decisions. The major obstacles to a land reform movement during the 1960s are not as prevalent at the local level as they are at any higher legislative level. It was the political power of the opponents to land reform—the owners of large tracts of land, the construction industry, and those who controlled a large amount of employment that made campaign contributions and provided the lobbying efforts—that prevented the land reform movement from gaining headway through legislative action. The political power of these groups is significantly less prevalent at the local level. Local constituencies simply have a much greater voice in local political decisions including land use issues. However, where local politicians are heavily influenced by a single individual, such as a large landowner or a firm that is economically important to the community, the influence of the individual or the firm will be prevalent.

The major thrust of the land reform movement at the local level has focused on residential development. To many developers putting land to its highest and best use means one thing, the maximum absolute density allowable on their parcel. While the private market will accommodate several types of neighborhoods, including some large-lot single-unit family housing neighborhoods, it is an inherent characteristic in the capitalistic system to capture economic rent. That is, when neighborhoods and communities create amenities above the average within a metropolitan area, it is natural for developers to take advantage of these amenities. It is in the process, however, that certain forms of development generate negative spillover effects for existing residents. As a consequence, residents have become increasingly involved in local land use decision making.[4]

This involvement has led to a prevailing view held by critics of existing land use policy in this country. In this view, as household growth occurs within a community, residents come to control politically all aspects of the community, including the planning commission or zoning board. In a sense, they become "the community" by virtue of their great numbers. The contention is that landowners with developable parcels are left with negligible political influence, and control over their property is established for the enjoyment of those who have political control, "the community" (Linowes and Allensworth 1973). Zoning, therefore, tends to offer communities, especially suburban communities, a highly favorable and inequitable distribution of entitlements to other people's property (Nelson 1977; Siegan 1972; Fischel 1978).

However, the obverse to this view can be posed in two ways. It may be that simply a change has occurred in the way in which society views the right to private property, especially urban property. Or it may be that the distrust in the market mechanism that culminated in the first passage of a zoning ordinance in 1916 is more deeply rooted than opponents to land use regulation have been able to grasp. Even Robert Nelson, who has long been an articulate opponent of zoning as a form of land use regulation, recognizes that "perhaps the greatest significance to the neighborhood movement lies in the challenge it poses to some widely accepted beliefs. The neighborhood movement shows a deep distrust of market institutions. The market is regarded as a destabilizing influence which erodes rather than sustains important social values'' (1984: 336). He goes on to say, however, that unlike traditional market antagonists, the neighborhood movement also shows a distrust of land use solutions by the local public sector. This issue will be addressed in chapter 5, but here it should be mentioned that by neighborhood, Nelson includes more than individual subdivisions or geographic areas of households, but substantially less than an entire community (political entity). The distinction is not particularly important. If the comprehensive plan has no statutory power, but if the elected officials who are ultimately responsible for any zoning change tend to follow the philosophy of the plan, then it seems apparent that a land reform movement has occurred at the local level, perhaps with lasting impact.

THE EXCLUSIONARY ARGUMENT AND THE COURTS

The current status of the judicial interpretation of land use regulation is far from clear. In Ramapo and Petaluma, the courts explicitly weighed the social implications of land use controls, and in both cases the courts found that the purposes of such controls to "ensure orderly growth" and "preserve the character of the community" outweighed the detrimental impacts on excluded residents. Although exclusionary zoning is a popular term in current land use literature, few state courts have discussed or addressed the issue. The courts that have addressed the issue, or at least partly addressed the issue, include Pennsylvania in 1965, New York in 1975, and California in 1976. However, none of the cases concerning exclusion in these states illustrates the issues and problems as well as the cases involving Mr. Laurel, New Jersey,[5] which are perhaps unlike any other land use cases during almost 80 years of zoning (Babcock and Siemon 1985: 207).

Mt. Laurel is a flat, sprawling township of 22 square miles, located 7 miles from Camden and 10 miles from the Benjamin Franklin Bridge crossing into Philadelphia. In 1950 the population was 2,817, only 600 more than in 1940. It was primarily rural and had no sizable settlements in 1950. By 1960 the population had doubled, and by 1970 it had doubled again to 11,221. The township was then part of the outer ring of the South Jersey Metropolitan Area.

Under the existing zoning ordinance adopted in 1964, 29.2 percent of all the land in the township, or 4,121 acres, was zoned for industry. At the time of the trial, no more than 100 acres were actually occupied by industrial uses. The amount of land zoned for retail was relatively small—169 acres or roughly 1.2 percent of the total land area. The remainder of the land area, almost 10,000 acres, had been developed, until recently, in the form of major subdivisions. The general ordinance provided for four residential zones, all of which permitted only single-family, detached dwellings with one house per lot. Attached town houses, apartments (except on farms for agricultural workers), and mobile homes were not allowed anywhere in the township. The general ordinance requirements, while not as restrictive as those in many similar municipalities, realistically allowed only homes that were within the financial reach of households of at least middle income.

Roughly one-half of the land zoned for residential use remained available for housing development, although the majority of it required a minimum lot size of one-half acre, somewhat larger than the minimum lot size in the areas already developed.

In 1967 Mt. Laurel adopted enabling legislation that permitted Planned Unit Development (PUD) projects. Although the ordinance was repealed in 1971, four PUD projects had been approved and were saved from extinction. For the first time, these projects did provide multiunit family housing in the form of rental garden, medium- and high-rise apartments, and attached town houses as well as single-family detached dwellings for sale. However, they were designed to be beyond the reach of low- and moderate-income families. For example, the township required that the developer must provide in its leases that no school-age children shall be permitted to occupy any one-bedroom apartment and that no more than two school-age children shall reside in any two-bedroom unit. In addition, in the event that more than three-tenths of a school child per multifamily unit attended the township school system in any one year, the developer will pay the cost of tuition and other school expenses of the excess number of children. These, along with other required amenities, clearly illustrate the intent to exclude low-income families.

In 1968 a nonprofit association sought to build subsidized, multifamily housing with funds granted by a higher level government agency. The Township Committee acknowledged the need for moderate-income housing in the area, but maintained that any housing must be constructed to all zoning and other applicable ordinances. This decision restricted construction to single-family detached dwellings on 20,000-square-foot lots.

The trial court in *Mt. Laurel I* invalidated the zoning ordinance in its entirety. It ordered the township to make certain studies and investigations and to present a plan to the court designed to enable and encourage the development of low- and moderate-income housing. The court concluded that every municipality must, by its land use regulations, make realistically possible an appropriate variety and choice of housing. It cannot eliminate the opportunity for low- and moderate-income housing, at least to the extent of the municipality's fair share of present and prospective regional need. A zoning regulation, like any police power enactment, must promote public health, safety, morals, or the general welfare. The universal and constant need for housing is so important and of such broad public interest that developing communities like Mt. Laurel must consider the general welfare that extends beyond their boundaries. Thus, a community must provide for its fair share of the region's moderate- and low-income housing.

There are obvious problems in implementing this decision. Primarily they involve what constitutes a community's fair share of low- and moderate-income housing, especially since the court stipulated that such housing be provided on a regional basis. In turn, it also meant that all communities need not provide some proportionate share so long as the need was being fulfilled on a regional basis. What then constitutes the region, and who was to define the appropriate region?

Most importantly, however, is that the root of the problem was not made an issue. It is an economic problem for which there is currently no solution that the private sector can provide. The major concern of those who argue that communities exclude through land use regulations is that the exclusion focuses on low-income families and therefore low-income housing. With absolutely no land regulation, the private sector cannot provide new low-income housing. As inexpensively as new housing can be constructed, even multiunit housing, it is out of the reach of low-income households. This we have long known.

The problems raised serious doubts about the *Mt. Laurel I* decision, and two years later (1977) the New Jersey Supreme Court engaged in a tactical retreat in the *Madison Township Decision*.[6] Here the court withdrew on two major fronts. First, it substituted "least cost" housing in place of housing for low- and moderate-income persons. Least cost thus meant the lowest priced housing that could be provided through the private market, meaning that new housing would not be provided for the urban poor. Here the argument was presented that more housing would be made available for the poor through the filtering process.

The second major retreat resulted from the recognition that the courts were sharply criticized for attempting to determine "fair share" of the regional need for low-income housing. The court conceded that this involves highly controversial economic, sociological, and policy questions and that trial courts were not competent to specify "fair share" and "pertinent region."

Further retreat from *Mt. Laurel I* is clearly evidenced in *Mt. Laurel II*. Following the first decision, Mt. Laurel began gathering information through its land planner to study the problem of exclusionary zoning and fair share plans, after which a new ordinance was adopted.

Criticisms of the new ordinance were extensive. In the first place, the new ordinance rezoned only 20 acres out of 14,300 acres to meet the requirements imposed by the court. Besides their inadequate size, the new zones had serious physical difficulties and restrictions created by the ordinance that rendered their actual development for low-cost housing virtually impossible. First, in the three zones created in the ordinance, each tract was owned by a single owner. Second, one of the zones was geographically isolated and so small that it was virtually unusable. Finally, impact studies must be made by the developer, although this was not required in the other zones.

Mt. Laurel countered by pointing out that the development of its PUD provided for multiunit family housing and that the filtering process would eventually generate low-income housing.

The court stipulated that this reasoning was statistical warfare, as in the Madison case, and it should be avoided. The court was simply unable to make a determination of Mt. Laurel's fair share. In the final analysis, the court thought Mt. Laurel had exercised its function in good faith and had complied with the intent of the court. One exception was that the court said Mt. Laurel should review a denial to develop a mobile home park.

Mt. Laurel I was directed at the urban poor, stating that they should have the right to live in suburbia with all its benefits. In the years that followed the poor fared no better. No low-income housing was built in suburbia. Moreover, there is an interesting, yet not unexpected, economic result. Because higher densities were permitted, developers tended to be the largest group of benefactors.

One aspect of the court's ruling in *Mt. Laurel II* generated significant criticism and litigation from many municipalities. Each community had an obligation to meet the need for lower income housing of the region, and the court suggested that 20 percent of any development would be adequate. Furthermore, a family should have to pay no more than 25 percent of its income for housing. It does not take much arithmetic to show that low- and moderate-income housing would have to be subsidized, and, given the court's ruling, it would be subsidized by future residents of any development. In effect, this form of subsidy is what has been termed "inclusionary zoning." There are many inherent problems to this type of housing subsidy, and they will be discussed in chapter 4.

While the Mt. Laurel cases illustrate many of the issues involved in what is termed exclusionary zoning, it should be kept in mind that zoning ordinances segregate uses of land and make differentiations even within use classifications. By their very nature they are exclusionary, hence, "exclusionary zoning" appears to be a somewhat redundant term. The use of it, however, tends to describe a form of economic segregation, with perhaps occasional racial overtones, that attempts to keep out lower income groups. If large minimum lot sizes are prescribed, if houses must contain some minimum amount of square feet, or if no multiunit family homes, mobile homes, or government-sponsored housing projects are permitted within a neighborhood or community, the result is the exclusion of a substantial segment of the population. The question is how exclusive can a community be without raising constitutional problems relating equal protection, due process, the right to travel, and similar issues?

Here the area of zoning law is still developing and presents conflicts. For example, five-acre, four-acre, and three-acre lot sizes have been upheld, but lot sizes of four acres and 100,000 square feet have been denied.[7] Moreover, it is not very likely that a consistent body of zoning law will emerge. Zoning law cases are primarily decided in state courts where there are substantial opportunities for vast differences in land use policy.

The cases in the 1970s have placed an entirely different focus on these problems. Rather than viewing them from the traditional perspective based on reasonableness under the police power, they have raised questions associated with civil rights cases. Current cases thus differ from earlier cases dealing with exclusion, not only on the legal issues involved but also with regard to the interests involved. *National Land* (1965, see note 7), for example, involved a challenge from developers. The more recent cases involved challenges from minorities or from agencies acting in their behalf. In addition to the Mt. Laurel decision in which there was an attempt to increase the availability of low-income housing, there have been supportive decisions such as *Hills v. Gautreaux* (1976). In this case the Supreme Court required the Chicago Housing Authority and the Department of Housing and Urban Development to utilize the entire Chicago metropolitan area, including the suburbs, to disperse low-income housing. This decision was another attempt to break down exclusionary barriers of the suburbs.

Again, in *Village of Arlington Heights I* (1977), the court stated that "discriminatory effect" was insufficient under the Fourteenth Amendment. A "discriminatory purpose" or intent was required to invalidate exclusionary suburban zoning. However, in *Arlington Heights II*,[8] the court concluded that the Village's refusal to rezone had a discriminatory effect. In *Arlington Heights III*,[9] the district court ultimately approved a compromise between the Metropolitan Housing Development Corporation (MHDC) and the Village of Arlington Heights. Arlington Heights, a predominantly white suburb, agreed to annex some currently unincorporated land (presumably controlled by MHDC) abutting the nearby Village of Mount Prospect. Arlington Heights pledged that for at least five years it would zone this land to permit multifamily and commercial uses. MHDC pledged, in turn, to build 190 units of subsidized rental housing and give the residents of Arlington Heights priority in occupancy. Both the Village of Mount Prospect and the owners of land near the site to be annexed objected, but the district judge approved the settlement. It was apparent, however, that despite the ruling of the Court, and in light of the current population of Arlington Heights, this plan obviously would not lead to much desegregation.

In 1987 the Supreme Court again ruled on a land use issue in *First English Evangelical Lutheran Church of Glendale, Appellant v. County of Los Angeles, California* that potentially could influence future local land use policy. Whether the ruling will have great significance is difficult to predict because, again, the court did not address the issue of what constitutes a taking. However, the decision made a major change in land use regulation. The First English Evangelical Lutheran Church of Glendale California owned 21 acres and several buildings in the Angeles National Forest on which it operated a campground known as "Luthergien" as a retreat center and recreation center for handicapped children. The land is located in a canyon along the banks of a creek that is the natural drainage channel for a watershed area. A forest fire in 1977 denuded the hills upstream from the campground and a storm the next year flooded the campground and destroyed its buildings. In response to the flood, Los Angeles County, in 1979, adopted an interim ordinance prohibiting the construction or reconstruction of any structure in an interim flood protection area.

Shortly after the ordinance was adopted a suit was filed alleging that the ordinance denied the church the use of Luthergien and seeking to recover damages. Heretofore, courts have upheld rulings that compensation is not required until the challenged regulation or ordinance has been held excessive, but the government nevertheless continues the regulation in effect. Hence, the California state courts held that the church could sue to overturn the ordinance but not to collect damages.

The Supreme Court ruled "where the government has 'taken' property by a land use regulation, the landowner may recover damages for the time before it is finally determined that the regulation constitutes a 'taking' of his property." The Court was, however, very clear to stipulate that temporary regulatory takings are not different in kind from permanent takings when they deny a landowner all use of his property. Denial of all use obviously constitutes a taking without due compensation. The grey area of how much regulation constitutes a taking remains for lower court decisions. The Court was aware that the ruling will lessen, to some extent, the freedom and flexibility of local governments in land use regulation. Dissenting opinions voiced fear that cautious local governments may avoid making any regulations that might be challenged and lead to damages, even in the area of health and safety.

At this writing, the opinion has just been made and its impact can not be analyzed. If the present philosophy toward land use policy that pervades many communities continues, as has been discussed and will be discussed again in chapter 5, an increased desire for managed growth will continue. Perhaps, as much as anything, the Supreme Court is sending a message with respect to exclusionary practices.

The court cases presented in this chapter by no means reflect the many cases in which courts have addressed the exclusionary issue. The cases are representative and among those most often cited. Thus it is clear that some courts have faced the exclusionary issue; yet it is just as apparent that no clear-cut doctrine involving exclusion has emerged. Perhaps a more clear doctrine will emerge with respect to exclusion than land use in general since the Supreme Court is more likely to be concerned with exclusionary issues.

CONCLUSION

In conclusion, two factors suggest that a land use reform movement did occur in the 1960s, and that a major thrust of the movement continued throughout the 1970s, and may actually be increasing. First, the Supreme Court has continued to support the right of people to reside in single-unit family neighborhoods, and in some state courts they have shown limited support for communities exercising greater control or management of growth and development at the local level. Second, while the land use reform of the 1960s had limited, if not dubious, success in the adoption and implementation of major changes in land use at the state level, the philosophy of the movement appears to have had significant impact at the local level.

While it is apparent that a land use reform movement has occurred in the United States through more stringent implementations of land use regulations at the local level, it may not, however, be correct to argue that a philosophical change toward land use has occurred. It could just as well be argued that the American attitude toward private property has remained pretty much as it always had been. Namely, the Constitution protects the right to private property. However, inherent in this right are two factors that sometimes conflict. One is the right to do as one pleases with owned property, including buying and selling land for a profit or buying, developing, and selling for a profit. Inherent in the right to private property is, however, an additional property right—a right that owned property has protection from negative spillovers of other property owners. Although some argue that the latter protection exists under nuisance law doctrine, courts have interpreted that there is some protective right inherent in the right to private property beginning with the first case upholding zoning as a legitimate exercise of police power.

It was not until the rapid urban growth and suburbanization of the post-World War II era that factors began to impinge upon the right to private property for the average American household, that is, the average household within an urban setting. As would be expected in a market economy, the private sector capitalized on existing amenities of neighborhoods in order to capture economic rents that resulted from land uses in proximity to these neighborhoods. Nelson (1984) thus views the land reform movement as the neighborhood movement. It is the neighborhood that now seems attractive because it offers virtues that may be threatened by modern society: cohesiveness of moral values, close personal ties, mutual trust, and stability. It is this which society desires to protect.

Whether there has indeed been a changing view toward society's meaning of the right to private property, or whether attitudes have changed very little, it is evident that households desire some control over land use within neighborhoods and even the community. The attitude is parochial, and it may generate exclusionary practices. Most apparent is that it is not a movement toward the notion that the right to private property is a right to do as one pleases with owned land.

Economists should be, and are, concerned with optimal land allocation. Should land be put to its highest and best use, that is, should an unfettered market prevail? Should land use be completely regulated? Is there some combination of the free market and regulation that will produce optimal land use? These are the questions that must be addressed. However, before proceeding to these questions, it is necessary to understand the administration and implementation of land use regulation.

NOTES

1. Transcript of Record (29,099) filed August 17, 1922, in the Supreme Court of the United States, October Term, 1922. P. 10. Id. P. 5., as quoted in Bosselman, Callies, and Banta (1973: 131).

2. 80 Cal. Rptr. at 905, citing *Miller v. Board of Public Works*, 234 P. 2d 381 at 383 (Bosselman, Callies, and Banta 1973: 215).

3. 89 Cal. Rptr. 906 (Bosselman, Callies, and Banta 1973: 217).

4. The concept of economic rent is discussed in detail in chapter 5.

5. There are two principal cases. The first, known as *Mt. Laurel I* is *Southern Burlington County NAACP v. Mount Laurel* (1975). The second case, referred to as *Mt. Laurel II*, is *Southern Burlington County NAACP v. Mount Laurel* (1983).

6. *Oakwood at Madison, Inc. v. Township of Madison* (1977). There are five or six additional cases that suggest a retreat from the *Mt. Laurel I* decision, although the Madison case is most often cited. See, for example, Babcock and Siemon (1985: 289).

7. See, for example, *County Commissioner's of Queen Anne's County v. Miles* (1967); *Flora Realty and Inv. Co. v. Ladue* (1952), appeal dismissed 344 U.S. 802 (1952); and *National Land and Inv. Co. v. Kohn* (1965).

8. *Metropolitan Housing Development Corp. v. Village of Arlington Heights* (1977).

9. *Metropolitan Housing Development Corp. v. Village of Arlington Heights* (1979).

2
The Administration and Implementation of Land Use Regulation

The reader must be aware that all states and even all communities within a particular state do not implement land use decisions in the same way. In reality, there may be as many different processes of implementation as there are local governments. Any attempt to provide a general description of land use implementation would have to be so general that it would be reduced to vague and sterile analysis.

It will become apparent, however, that in chapter 3 the process of implementing land use decisions is an important aspect of the economic and legal rationale for developing a model for optimal land use. It is imperative, therefore, that we understand how land use regulation is implemented, at least in many communities throughout the nation. This chapter describes the process of implementation for a particular suburban community, although the process is representative of many communities with minor variations. Few generalities are made throughout the chapter, but those familiar with the process of implementation in various communities will be able to make appropriate adjustments. For example, the differences in the manner in which noncontroversial and controversial land use issues are made are presented in two sections. There are, however, some communities in which all zoning changes may be controversial. Note that for the purpose of this discussion the major interest is in the actual implementation, although a brief background of statutory provisions is necessary.

FEDERAL AND STATE CONTROLS

The major federal law concerning land use issues is the National Environmental Policy Act (NEPA). This act requires federal agencies to conduct environmental impact analyses for development activities such as airport development, low-income housing, and transportation infrastructure. Communities then have the opportunity to review the studies and object to them if they so desire. NEPA is also used by members of a community, such as environmentalists, to attempt to block or redirect certain types of development. If a compromise is not reached, challenges may end up in court where opponents may gain concessions or even stop the project.

Certain federal agencies have a variety of regulations that pertain to land use including soil conservation, mining, forestry, navigable waterways, and air- and waterways. These are important in that they affect large quantities of land and many economic activities. They are neglected here, however, because they do not have a significant influence on local land use. The major exception would be noise related to air traffic.

The changing attitude toward land use that arose in the early 1960s did eventually lead to actions by a few state legislatures (most notably Oregon and Vermont) to establish statewide regional land use commissions. Similar commissions were established in other states, but only for a particular area of the state such as New York's Adirondack Park Agency and the California Coastal Commission. In addition, metropolitan federations have been established to coordinate land use policies among the local governments that constitute large urban areas. The Minneapolis and St. Paul Metropolitan Council is a well-known example.

Despite these attempts, these new agencies have done little to supplant local autonomy. Local governments are very reluctant to relinquish control over land use decisions. As has been pointed out (Callies 1980), there have been few initiatives toward proenvironment land use controls since about 1976. This is not surprising given the difficulty encountered by the proenvironmentalists at the state level during the 1960s and 1970s. However, as was pointed out in chapter 1, a proenvironmentalist view combined with a managed growth philosophy is evident in the land reform movement at the local level.

STATUTORY AUTHORITY FOR ZONING

The statutory authorization for zoning by local government normally derives from enabling legislation passed by the state legislature. Occasionally the authority has come from home rule charter provisions or state constitutional amendments. In Georgia and New Jersey, where the state courts initially held zoning to be unconstitutional, the constitutions were amended in order to make zoning legal. As a result of the widespread adoption of the Standard State Zoning Enabling Act (SZEA) in 1926 (see chapter 1), the statutory authorization for zoning was remarkably similar for many years throughout the United States. Most states either adopted legislation that was taken verbatim from SZEA or was heavily influenced by it. Perhaps just as surprising is the durability of the act—in many states it has lasted over 50 years with only minor changes.

The popularity for the SZEA is probably attributable to the broad and vaguely defined powers that it grants to local governments. Many commentators agree there appears to be no better way to convey the sense of these powers than to simply reprint the first three sections of the act.

Section 1. Grant of Power—For the purpose of promoting health, safety, morals, or the general welfare of the community, the legislative body of cities and incorporated villages is hereby empowered to regulate and restrict the height, number of stories, and size of buildings and other structures, the percentage of lot that may be occupied, the size of yards, courts, and other open spaces, the density of population, and the location and use of buildings, structures, and land for trade, industry, residence, or other purposes.

Section 2. Districts—For any or all of said purposes the local legislative body may divide the municipality into districts of such number, shape, and area as may be deemed best suited to carry out the purposes of this act; and within such districts it may regulate and restrict the erection, construction, reconstruction, alteration, repair, or use of buildings, structures, or land. All such regulations shall be uniform for each class or kind of buildings throughout each district, but the regulations in one district may differ from those in other districts.

Section 3. Purposes in View—Such regulations shall be made in accordance with a comprehensive plan and designed to lessen congestion in the streets; to secure safety from fire, panic, and other dangers; to promote health and the general welfare; to provide adequate light and air; to prevent the overcrowding of land; to avoid undue concentration of population; to facilitate the adequate provision of transportation, water, sewerage, schools, parks, and other public requirements. Such regulations shall be made with reasonable consideration, among other things, to the character of the district and its peculiar suitability for particular uses, and with a view to conserving the value of buildings and encouraging the most appropriate use of land throughout such municipality.

The broad powers of authority in Section 1 are apparent. Whether the authors of SZEA recognized the breadth of the powers that would be granted to localities is difficult to ascertain. They clearly include the notion of "fiscal zoning." It is just as clear that the rapid adoption of zoning ordinances (chapter 1) suggests a widespread desire by localities to achieve some control over land use, a control that stemmed from nonconforming uses of land leading to negative spillovers. Moreover, this remains the fundamental reason behind the present attitude toward land use regulation at the local level.

It is true that state enabling acts and local ordinances are not as uniform as they were in the past. This may be partly attributable to changes necessary to include the regional authorities. More importantly, the changes have come about in response to political and lobbying pressures at the local level. These pressures have resulted in wide differences in density requirements among communities as well as new zoning devices such as a Planned Unit Development, cluster housing, and zero lot line construction. Consequently, through time local zoning ordinances have and will continue to differ significantly.

THE ADMINISTRATION OF LAND USE REGULATION

In all communities land regulation began with zoning, which is the division of the community into districts in which certain activities are prohibited and others are permitted. The establishment of zoning ordinances and changes in these ordinances are the responsibility of the local governing body. Administrative and minor adjustments are delegated to the planning commission and some can be administratively accomplished by the planning staff. Members of the planning commission are usually appointed by the governing body, though occasionally their office may be elective. In addition, variances to the local ordinance can be granted by the Zoning Board of Adjustments (the official title varies by state, but it is normally referred to as the ZBA), which is also appointed by the local governing body. In practice, the ZBA has a very minor role in the overall process in most communities.

The planning commission has two primary functions: first, it acts in an advisory capacity to the governing body with respect to major land use decisions, including zoning changes and the development and updates of the comprehensive plan; and second, it implements the regulations of the ordinances with respect to subdivision regulations and site plans. In addition, the planning commission, in conjunction with the staff, makes recommendations to the governing body with respect to the need and geographic location of future infrastructure, which would also be an aspect of the comprehensive plan.

Subdivision and Site Regulations

Within any zoning ordinance there are several subsets of ordinances that primarily delineate what cannot be developed within a specific zone. There may be several residential zones with varying degrees of density requirements ranging from single-unit family housing to high-density multiunit family housing, two or three types of commercial and industrial zones, and two or three types of agricultural zones that also permit certain types of development. Within each zone builders are subject to specific regulations. In order to proceed with their projects, builders must meet the requirements of the ordinance for the specific zone. These may include regulations that the developer install the infrastructure within the development, including roads, culverts, sewer and water lines, all constructed to certain specifications. They may also include setbacks, natural screening, or a specific number of parking spaces per square foot of developed space or number of developed units. Most ordinances also now include PUDs, which permit a wide variety of development within a single parcel including commercial, industrial, and the full range of residential housing. Here the community is essentially concerned with the gross density of development within the PUD and does not regulate each type of development within the PUD. Under each of these regulations, developers must bear certain costs, but having met the regulations developers normally have the right to develop their parcels.

Building and Housing Codes

Building codes are rather straightforward in that they simply designate the standards for materials and the procedures to be followed in the construction of new housing and neighborhood infrastructure. They require minimum standards for such things as foundation footings and the materials and installation of electrical, heating, and plumbing facilities. These are clearly necessary in today's society to anyone who is familiar with construction. Even though the majority of all contractors would adhere to the minimum standards, there are a few who would not. Some of these regulations may add to the cost of any structure and, in some cases, they have been criticized for retarding technological change in construction (Colwell and Kau 1982). Studies to date do not suggest, however, that these effects on housing costs have been significant (Muth and Wetzler 1976).

It may be that the construction industry has failed to be very innovative. For example, with only minor exceptions, single-unit family housing is constructed in the same way today as it was 50 or more years ago. Lack of innovation is obviously one reason why the cost of housing has increased relative to the cost of other goods. Yet an argument can be made that the construction industry may not have been at fault. A major reason that the relative price of many goods has declined over the past several decades is attributable to two factors. First, we were able to take advantage of large economies of scale attributable to Western technology; and second, innovative improvements in production were more readily adaptable to large-scale production. It seems entirely plausible that large-scale production of housing would have produced a fall in the relative price of housing just as it did in the automobile industry. Yet the answer is obvious: While there may be large economies of scale in the production of housing that we have not been able to reap, we have not been able to overcome the cost of transportation in the housing industry.

THE IMPLEMENTATION OF LAND USE REGULATION

In addition to providing the reader with a description of how land use regulations are implemented, this section serves two other purposes. First, it provides some insight into the politics involved in the regulatory process. Second, the way in which land use policy and land use regulations are implemented sets the stage for the model presented in chapter 3. If our models conform fairly closely to reality, we are in a much better position to use the model as a way of demonstrating how changes can lead to a more optimal allocation of resources. Recognizing that land allocation can be improved, an understanding of how it works is necessary before realistic attempts for improvement can be offered.

The Comprehensive Plan

Section 3 of the SZEA states that zoning shall be done in accordance with a comprehensive plan. If planning for land use is desirable, then clearly this is the correct approach. The comprehensive plan would document the goals of the community, and these goals would be implemented through zoning. That is, the zones for land use would conform to the plan. But, recall that it did not work this way. Zoning came first. Most communities did not begin to develop comprehensive plans for growth and development until the 1960s, and many rural communities have yet to develop a plan. It is interesting, however, that several states have required each locality to adopt a comprehensive plan and, through state and federal subsidies, provided funds for professional planners to those localities that had no professional planning staff.

Commentators on the movement toward encouraging a more formal planning process suggest that there were conflicting motives behind the movement (Mandelker 1976; Tarlock 1975). One concern was that zoning ordinances were not sufficiently restrictive in that they were not designed to preclude long-range detrimental effects of growth. Conversely, there was the concern that zoning was too restrictive—the exclusionary argument. Some states thus adopted legislation that attempted to force communities to become less restrictive.

There were merits to each argument, but, for those suburban communities in the path of urban growth, the comprehensive plan provided the means to address a fundamental concern at the local level. Because zoning came first, and in order to appease both the landowners of undeveloped land and suburbanites, the initial layout of zones, and often the uses within those zones, did not conform to either a plan for development or any goals for development, if any existed. The comprehensive plan thus provided a means for local communities to develop some consistency between zoning and planning. It was, in effect, the beginning of a process to alleviate continual conflicts between landlord-developers and some rational plan for future growth. Once the plan was set out, although it was not laid in concrete, it provided the private sector with a general idea of how certain parcels of land could and could not be used. Each parcel of land is zoned for a specific use, including an agricultural zone that usually permits several types of development. However, as the community develops, many land owners envisage future uses of their parcels that are not consistent with existing zoning. It is through the comprehensive plan that landowners are able to predict, with some degree of accuracy, the future uses of their parcels. Perhaps more than any other factor this was a major impetus behind the adoption of comprehensive plans, especially in those communities in the path of rapid urban growth. It was a logical extension of the quiet revolution in land reform that began in the early 1960s.

THE COMPREHENSIVE PLAN AND ZONING: NONCONTROVERSIAL ISSUES

The stage is now set: How does the land regulation process work for most communities? If an owner wishes to develop land in a way that is consistent with both the comprehensive plan and the zoning ordinance, the process is simple. The following provides an illustration of the process in a representative community. The developer presents a set of plans, usually drafted to scale by an engineer, to the planning staff of the administration. The staff reviews the plans and presents the case to a subcommittee of the planning commission: a subdivision review committee for residential use or a site plan review committee for commercial or industrial use. The landlord-developer or a representative, usually the engineer who drafted the plans, also attends the presentation. In the presentation of the case, the staff will include comments and recommendations of the highway department and the public health department. Here the staff may have minor comments for changes that are needed to meet the letter of an ordinance that are usually acceptable to the landlord-developer. But no ordinance is perfect for all situations. If the landlord-developer has sound reasons for objecting to a minor change, the commission members of the subcommittee may, and often do, override a staff recommendation. These cases are then entered on the agenda of the next meeting of the planning commission. They are rarely discussed at the planning commission meeting and are passed by the full commission with the recommendation of the staff and the subcommittee.

Some zoning changes are also relatively noncontroversial to the general public, the planning commission, and the governing body in many communities throughout the nation. It is probably true, however, that in every community practically any zoning change may bring controversy from adjacent property owners or the landlord-developer if the requested change is denied. Zoning changes usually require two public hearings, one before the planning commission and one before the governing body. Zoning changes do not go through a subcommittee but come directly before the commission. Most noncontroversial zoning changes are those in which the requested change requires a rezoning of a land parcel to conform to the comprehensive plan or a denial of a request to rezone to a use that is not consistent with the plan. The staff presents the case to the commission with its recommendation. Following the presentation, in some communities, a representative of the landlord-developer requesting the change, often an attorney but sometimes the landowner, presents their case for the requested change. The public is then invited to speak. In other communities, the public may be invited to speak first. In noncontroversial zoning changes, the commission normally accepts the recommendation of the staff that is forwarded to the governing body. At the next meeting of the governing body the same process is reenacted. It should also be noted that there are many rezonings that do not conform to the comprehensive plan, yet they are noncontroversial. The plan is not perfect and when reasonable requests for rezonings are made that are not consistent with the plan, they are often noncontroversial.

Again, the reader should be aware that this description of how the process works may be applicable to only one community. However, some combination of this section and the following section describes a process that is representative of how land use decisions are implemented in many communities.

THE COMPREHENSIVE PLAN AND ZONING: CONTROVERSIAL ISSUES

Controversial zoning issues are significantly more important for purpose of discussion. We must understand how they get resolved but, more importantly, how their resolution relates to the model and the implementation of the model in Chapter 3. In order to understand the process, it will be helpful to understand the nature of the conflict that gives rise to controversial land use issues. We can begin with the premise that, except when the market for land development will not support it, most landlord-developers will attempt to build out at the highest density level permissible within the zone of their land parcel. Moreover, in requests for rezoning, "rent seeking" is one of the motives often observed in the behavior of landlord-developers. (See chapter 5 for a discussion of land rent.) This simply reflects normal behavior in a market system. Simultaneously, it is this behavior that often leads to negative spillovers, which lead to the conflict between landlord-developers and members of local communities.

Common Conflicts in a Controversial Zoning Issue

The more common conflicts between the "community" in a suburban setting and landlord-developers include the following categories: aggregate population density, site-specific population density, site-specific commercial density, transportation, and environmental issues. The concern over aggregate population density is, in effect, a reflection of a concern to maintain the ambience of the community. People choose to reside in a particular neighborhood in a particular community for a variety of reasons, one of the more important being the ambience of the neighborhood and the community. These residents, in general, are not opposed to growth throughout the community since they understand that the character of a community in the path of urban growth will change. Any significant growth will change the character of a community. They are, however, concerned about maintaining the ambience of the community; they want the community to remain suburban as opposed to becoming urban. And, without becoming embroiled in the issue of property rights at this stage, these residents perceive that they have some right in maintaining the ambience of the community. This simply implies that the community retain a suburban setting as opposed to an urban, or more densely populated, setting.

Site-specific population density concerns normally arise when landlord-developers desire to develop a neighborhood with significantly higher density levels adjacent to neighborhoods with lower levels of density. The typical illustration is the construction of apartments adjacent to single-unit family residential neighborhoods. Residents generally do not oppose the development of multiunit family neighborhoods, such as condominiums, town houses, and cluster housing, so long as the gross density levels of the parcel to be developed are fairly consistent with that of the adjacent neighborhoods. In addition, residents do not generally oppose site-specific development of high-density housing so long as it does not generate a negative spillover that directly affects their neighborhood.

Site-specific commercial development normally does not concern the general populace unless it abuts a residential neighborhood. This concern generally emanates from the planning staff and the planning commission. The major concern is whether adequate infrastructure is or can be made available. Developers are usually aware of this information, or it is available in the comprehensive plan. Nevertheless, requests for rezoning occur in areas where the infrastructure is inadequate and will not be available for some time. Minor conflicts between the landlord-developer and the staff or members of the commission usually involve setbacks, screening, parking space, and occasionally design aesthetics. In a community in which rapid growth is occurring, a major problem in planning for commercial growth is some attempt to control strip-type development. Long-range goals for adequate transportation such as service roads or the availability of land for future widening of the main artery can conflict with current land use desires of landowners.

Transportation concerns may create opposition from both planners and residents. We all know the fundamental problem: Main artery routes are never built to handle all of the traffic that will be generated by full development of a section of the community. In many suburban communities, the main arteries were constructed to accommodate rural traffic, not suburban traffic. Consequently, bottlenecks and inadequate road service often occur rather early in the development stage. Two factors exacerbate the conflict. First, suburban communities are often within counties rather than a city, and the transportation infrastructure for counties may be provided by the state, or by the metropolitan government, but not the local government. Consequently, the decision as to when and where to upgrade the existing system or to add to the infrastructure is not made by the local government. For those communities that do not provide their own transportation infrastructure, upgrading the road system often does not occur until the existing road system equals or exceeds capacity.

There is, moreover, an additional conflict that results from the transportation issue. One advantage of suburban living is the lack of congestion relative to the central city. As a consequence, the criteria for the capacity of the road system for suburban residents are significantly less than the criteria of the state or the municipality providing the system. Residents, therefore, feel that at some stage of development in their section of the community, future growth will generate congestion by suburban standards that will not be alleviated. In order to attempt to prevent future congestion, landlord-developers may be required to provide more road infrastructure than they believe necessary or, at least, they may be required to set aside land for future road development or provide setbacks for future widening of the road system.

The environmental issue simply involves the conflict over how much and what type of development can occur in environmentally sensitive land areas. More recently, the conflict has spread to how much and what type of development can occur in watershed areas for reservoirs, which can include relatively large land areas.

Resolving Controversial Zoning Issues

The administrative process of all zonings, controversial or noncontroversial, is identical. The outcome of a controversial issue is influenced, however, by several factors: the project itself, the planning staff, the planning commission, the residents of the community, and the local governing body. The proposal for a rezoning is initially submitted to the planning staff, which is required to review the proposal and submit staff recommendations to the planning commission within a specified time frame. The proposal is not simply a request for a rezoning; rather, it normally is a proposal that includes some or many specifics of the proposed development. If it is a residential proposal, it would include lot sizes, street layouts of at least the initial phases of the project, if not all phases, and open space areas. This would hold for various types of residential use from single-unit family housing to multiunit or mixed development.

An important aspect of the process occurs in the review by the planning staff. The staff's recommendations will be heavily influenced by the comprehensive plan. So long as the project conforms to the uses of land as indicated by the comprehensive plan, the recommendation by the staff will probably be favorable. If not, the recommendation will very likely be one of denial. This will become an important consideration in the model in chapter 3, because even though the comprehensive plan does not bear legal sanction, as does zoning, it is increasingly being implemented as if it does.

The members of the commission and the landlord-developer receive the report of the staff only a few days (sometimes one or two) prior to the regularly scheduled meeting of the commission. If the staff recommendation is one of denial, the landlord-developer has three courses of action.

One course of action is to persuade the members of the commission that the development is in the best interest of the community. Even though the staff recommendation has been to deny the zoning change on the grounds that it is not consistent with the comprehensive plan, an argument can be made that the development is consistent with surrounding growth, which is to suggest that it is time to make adjustments in the comprehensive plan. If it is a relatively large development, the presentation by the developer will include a cost-benefit analysis and transportation study in an attempt to show the positive impacts and to minimize the negative impacts both for the community and adjacent property owners. Developers also frequently demonstrate the employment impact generated by their project including the multiplier effects of commercial and industrial growth. If the project is reasonable and if there are minimal negative comments from interested parties, the commission may recommend approval of the rezoning request to the governing body.

Suppose, however, that it appears to the developer that the rezoning will be denied by the commission. Actually, this can occur at two different times. First, given the staff report, it may be obvious that the commission will approve the report, that is, a recommendation to deny the request. However, the intent of the commission may not become apparent to the developer until after the public hearing, at which time all interested parties have had a chance to voice their concerns, and after the members of the commission have discussed the case, but before a vote is taken.

In a majority of these cases, the conflict arises because the landlord-developer has requested the maximum density allowable in the rezoning. For example, if it is a request for rezoning from single-unit family housing to multiunit housing, the design of the project is for the maximum allowable density in the multiunit family zone. If it appears that the project would be acceptable to the members of the commission but only at a lower number of multifamily units than the maximum allowable, the landlord-developer may request to withdraw the proposal with the intent of resubmitting at the next meeting. The landlord-developer will then redesign the project to include fewer units. In order to obtain the rezoning, at the next meeting, the landlord-developer will proffer that a given number of units will be constructed in order to obtain the rezoning. The proffer is permanent in that it is attached to property.

A proffer is relatively new to the process and may not exist in many communities. In essence, the developer stipulates, in a written agreement, a maximum amount of development that will be placed on the parcel of land for which the rezoning is being requested. The proffer is binding and is attached to the deed of the land. A proffer must originate from the landlord-developer. It is illegal for the staff, planning commission, or governing body to request a specific proffer. Although a proffer is relatively new, conditional zoning and special use permits have long been used by most communities as a means of ensuring maximum density, height, or other restrictions on the development of a particular parcel.

But why should the developer be denied permission to develop at the maximum density permitted by the zoning ordinance? For example, if the multiunit family zone permits the development of up to 12 units per acre, why should the developer not be permitted to construct 12 units, yet 6 or 8 might be acceptable. First, the site itself may have unique terrain features that would create environmental or transportation problems if developed to the maximum permitted. A zoning ordinance simply cannot be written that applies equally to all land parcels—no zoning ordinance is perfect. Second, and perhaps more important, in the evolutionary growth of the community, residents of the suburban community desire to protect the ambience of the community. Multiunit family densities of 6 per acre may protect the ambience in one section of the community while 12 per acre would not change the ambience in a different section. This may depend upon transportation facilities, the nature of surrounding neighborhoods, or other factors unique to the parcel.

This has been but one illustration. Proffers, conditional zoning, or special use permits may take many forms and apply to all types of projects including commercial and industrial. They may include devoted rights-of-way for future roads, setbacks from sensitive environmental lands, or the donation of lands for public facilities in addition to specifying levels of density.

The PUD has also been increasing in importance as a way in which the developer and the community authorities negotiate specific features of a project. PUDs are normally only appropriate for large tracts of land and contain a wide mixture of development. There are two major virtues to PUDs. While they allow for more community involvement and direction in the project, the developer is also in a better position to bargain with the community authorities. In addition, the specific geographical layout of the entire PUD is not necessary in the initial stages of the project. That is, gross density levels are initially set out, but the net density levels of particular types of development can be left to the discretion of the developer.

The landlord-developer always has a third alternative. The project can be withdrawn at any stage, or the project can go through the entire process and either be approved or denied by the governing body. It is important to recognize that the governing body is, by far, the most important factor in the process. While there may have been some hope that urban planning was to be removed from partisan politics and pressures and to become part of the technocratic process (Nelson 1977), this has not occurred. Despite the recommendations of the planning staff and those of the planning commission, the governing body has the final responsibility for all zoning changes, conditional zoning, special use permits, and the acceptance of proffers.

At this stage in the process, one of two factions comes into play. One is that the political power of landlord-developers is so influential among members of the governing body that their interests are predominantly served. Conversely, politics is found in site-specific requests for zoning changes. These involve issues in which residents of a neighborhood(s) perceive that a change in zoning will generate a negative spillover in their neighborhood. In some of these cases, the residents have not been able to convince either the planning staff or the planning commission that the spillovers are sufficient to deny the request, yet they are able to convince their local politicians at public hearings.

THE SIGNIFICANCE OF THE PROCESS

It is important to emphasize the purpose of this discussion. The process illustrates several significant features of land use regulation as it is currently implemented in many suburban communities. First, zoning should be flexible, not rigid. A perfect zoning ordinance cannot be written that applies to each parcel of land. Negotiations and deals between the public sector and the landlord-developer provide the necessary flexibility.

The process also illustrates that mediation and deals do occur between the landlord-developer and the public sector. Because growth and development are evolutionary, it is through the mediation process, combined with a comprehensive plan, that landlord-developers are in a position to predict the use of underdeveloped land parcels in the community. As a consequence, in order to facilitate the administration of their requests through the process, the initial requests are more and more presented in a way that is acceptable to the governing body.

Although the tone of this discussion suggests that the public sector often attempts to limit development, the reader should bear in mind that this portion of the discussion has focused on controversial land use issues. These are the controversies that arise when the landlord-developer has requested land use densities that exceed what normally might be expected. Since many types of development are desired, they are noncontroversial.

3
A Model for Optimal Land Use

Chapter 2 presented a process for land use decision making and the implementation of land use policy as currently exists for a community in the United States. Although the exact process described may apply to only one or a few communities, variations of the process reflect that of many, if not most, communities. As previously stated, it is the process itself that is important. It is important for two reasons. One, it is the process and the allocation of land that results from the process that has given rise to harsh criticisms of land use regulation, especially zoning as a form of regulation. More importantly, a major purpose of this chapter is to develop a model that is applicable to the process of developing and implementing land use policy. As stated earlier, if changes are needed in order to approach optimal land use, they must come from within the existing institutional structure.

A theoretical model for optimal land use has been provided by J. V. Henderson (1980). The section in this chapter entitled "A Description of a Theoretical Model of Optimal Land Use" is, in effect, a verbal description of Henderson's model. The theoretical model differs from previous models in that it is dynamic as opposed to being static. Since land use is dynamic, that is, land use evolves through time, Henderson's analysis is more applicable to real-world situations. Nevertheless, the model contains some assumptions that make it difficult to apply in an analysis of land use. One of the assumptions is that, for optimal land use to occur, a binding agreement or a contract must be formed between the residents of a community and the landlord-developer between two time periods. That is, those who purchase land in time period one must have a contract that gives them some assurance of what the community will be like in time period two in order to know the value of land in time period one. Otherwise, they cannot attain their highest utility level. Two factors prohibit forming this type of contract. First, landlord-developers do not own all of the land in a community; therefore, they cannot contract with residents for land that is not theirs. Second, new landlord-developers can enter the community in time period two.

There is, however, an interesting solution to the formation of the contract between two time periods. In effect, the solution provides the link between the theoretical model and the process of land use implementation in the United States. Once the link between the theoretical model and the process of implementation is provided, a model that will approach optimal land use can be developed.

The major reason for adopting zoning as a form of land use regulation is to prevent negative spillovers. However, many critics of zoning contend that the negative spillover argument has been overrated. As a consequence, land use regulation has led to exclusionary practices in many localities. Therefore, before developing a model for optimal land use, the negative spillover argument should be addressed.

THE NEGATIVE SPILLOVER ARGUMENT

Land use regulation, especially zoning as a form of regulation, has been increasingly attacked by economists as being less efficient and less equitable in the allocation of land than the free market solution.[1] The predominant argument stems from a mercantilist notion reflecting parochial community interest. As a consequence, localities exercise exclusionary land use controls that result in lower levels of density in housing units than would obtain in the free market. In this section, the theoretical model illustrating the effect of negative spillovers that result from noncompatible uses of land is presented followed by a summary of attempts to verify the empirical impact of negative spillovers.

The Theoretical Model

There is widespread agreement among economists that social intervention in private markets is not warranted unless the markets are not functioning efficiently. It is generally conceived, therefore, that the widespread acceptance for public intervention in the market for land is attributable to the existence of negative spillover effects. Hence, by segregating nonconforming land uses through regulation, the allocation of land is both more efficient and more equitable than would obtain in the free market.

Following the work of David Mills (1979), this notion is demonstrated in the following model. Given the existence of negative spillovers, a zoning policy is optimal if, through zoning, land is utilized in a way that is both socially efficient and equitable. A state of the world is socially efficient if it maximizes monetary benefits. Since this criterion implicitly endorses a social welfare function that values an increase in monetary benefits the same for each member of society, a decision or policy that assumes an equal monetary return to owners of identical land parcels is equitable.

Whether zoning can produce optimal land use is, to a large extent, dependent upon the characteristic of the negative spillover, specifically the persistent or nonpersistent nature of the spillover. A persistent spillover is one that would not be greatly affected by changing the location of land uses that produce or receive the spillover; smog is an excellent example. A nonpersistent spillover, however, may be totally eliminated by separating the producing and receiving land uses, for example, visual and noise-related activities. While, realistically, spillovers fall along a persistence continuum, the following analysis deals exclusively with spillovers that are nonpersistent.

Utilizing figure 1, with units of land plotted on the horizontal axis and units of value vertically, total land in the community is OL with residential use noted by L_1, and the balance L_1L used commercially. D_r is the demand for residential land, and it is segregated from commercial use. The demand for commercial land, D_c, is juxtaposed on the graph, that is, plotted left to right. D'_r reflects the impact of negative spillovers created by commercial use on the demand for residential land. D^{∂}_r is thus the demand for land for residential use when each parcel is adjacent to a commercial parcel. The magnitude of the external diseconomy imposed on each nonsegregated residential land use is ab. Using the consumer surplus approach, the socially efficient zoning policy that maximizes aggregate monetary benefits is measured by the sum of the areas under the demand curves. Therefore, OL_1 units of land must be allocated to residential and L_1L to a commercial zone. Any other allocation of land would generate a loss in benefits from one use that exceeds the gain in the other. If there are no boundary effects (that is, if the commercial use of land does not generate negative spillovers at the common boundary), external diseconomies are completely eliminated by segregation. Land use is thus socially efficient.

Figure 1
Land Use and Negative Spillovers

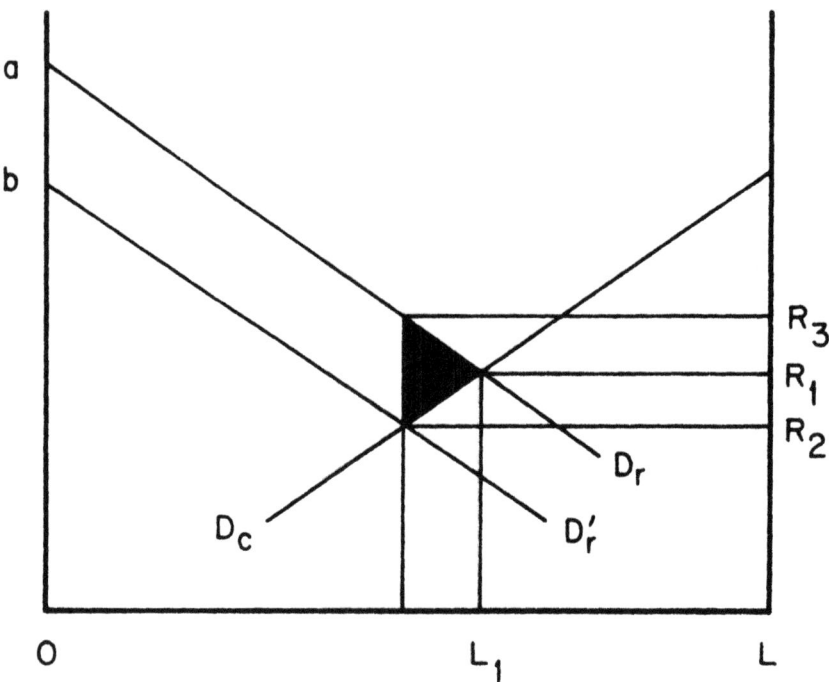

Source: Compiled by the author.

The policy is also equitable since the rent on land throughout the community is R_1, the intersection of supply and demand for each use. This coincidence of social efficiency and equity thus assures the existence of an optimal zoning policy.

It is possible for segregation to occur naturally. Nevertheless, efficient land use will result only if there are no boundary effects between the "natural zones." If boundary effects do exist, natural segregation will cause the boundary to be misplaced. Consequently, too much land will be used commercially and too little put into residential use for the result to be socially efficient or equitable. This result is illustrated in figure 1. Given the existence of diseconomies, without zoning the rental rate for land is equal on both sides of the boundary, at R_2, the intersection of the demand for commercial and the demand for residential land on the boundary. But, because of the boundary effect, the rental rate for residential land on the boundary is R_2, which is less than that inside the boundary. R_3 reflects the price for residential land inside the boundary. The amount of land in the residential zone is less and the amount of land in the commercial zone is more than would be obtained in the absence of the boundary effect. As a result, this is neither a socially efficient nor equitable use of land. It is socially inefficient since the total area under the demand curves is less by the size of the shaded area (that is, compared with the equilibrium absent boundary effects), and it is inequitable because the rental rate differs among homogeneous land parcels.

This analysis thus suggests the potential for regulation as a means of enhancing social benefit. That is, given the existence of boundary effects, a scheme for allocating land use could be implemented to produce both a more socially efficient and a more equitable use of land than would be obtained in the free market. To a large extent, this allocation is already effectively accomplished in most communities through existing regulations. Communities commonly separate commercial, industrial, and residential areas in order to minimize the effect of negative spillovers. Both natural and man-made boundaries are often utilized. Where plans for future growth have been developed, landowners are aware of the type of development that is likely to occur on given land parcels, which further serves to minimize future negative spillovers. In addition, existing and future infrastructure construction further segregates major categories of land use both through regulation and the free market. That is, the planning and implementation of infrastructure, which in effect is a form of regulation, must be complemented with the uses of land if optimal utilization of land, including infrastructure, is to occur.

THE EMPIRICAL EVIDENCE

Critics of zoning contend, however, that the impact of negative externalities has been overrated. This hypothesis has been tested in several studies by ascertaining the impact of negative spillovers on housing value. In the seminal study of Pittsburgh by Crecine, Davis, and Jackson (1967), the basic results provide no systematic evidence to indicate that the value of single-family housing was negatively affected by nonconforming land uses within the immediate neighborhood. Their analysis further suggests that land use externalities may be very localized; they are essentially "next door" phenomena. Rueter's (1973) effort to refine the data for the Pittsburgh study has produced similar results. Both studies conclude that the effects of spillovers vary in magnitude and direction across zoning categories and census tracts, suggesting that what may be a diseconomy for one area produces an economy for another area. Maser, Riker and Rosett's (1977) study of Monroe County, New York, which includes Rochester, also finds that the diversity of tastes among buyers is sufficient for the market to find those who are indifferent to uses of land that may be offensive to others. These studies thus suggest that land use regulation is not justified by the presence of negative spillovers, and that the allocative efficiency of zoning is not effective. These results were further corroborated by Grether and Mieszkowski (1974) in their attempt to determine whether the value of a house increases as a function of distance from a nonconforming land use. For most zones they could not demonstrate a consistent increase in the value of houses further removed from a nonconforming land use.

The results of other empirical studies, however, contrast sharply with the preceding findings. First, it should be pointed out that the results of the studies for Pittsburgh and Monroe County are not especially surprising given the definition of "neighborhood" in each study. In the Crecine, Davis, and Jackson study, "neighborhood" is defined to be the home's city block, while Rueter defines "neighborhood" as either a 150-foot radius or a 300-foot radius from the home. Maser, Riker, and Rosett defined "neighborhood" to include property on either side or directly across the street in order to include other land visible from the observed parcel. As has been pointed out by Lafferty and Frech (1978), these definitions of the relevant neighborhood are too simple.

Uses of certain parcels of land within a metropolitan area generate two types of spillovers or spillovers at two levels. First, commercial and industrial uses generate positive spillovers for the metropolitan area by enhancing the level of economic activity, revenue base, and economic opportunities for residents. These types of spillovers pervade the entire metropolitan area. The second level of spillovers affects relatively short distances, these being the neighborhood effects. This view, therefore, is consistent with the traditional rationale for zoning. If, through zoning, larger neighborhoods have been protected relatively well from negative spillovers of noncompatible land uses, it is understandable that external effects would not be found in those studies that used small neighborhoods.

In a study of 40 suburban towns in the Boston metropolitan area, William Stull (1975) uses the proportion of a community's land devoted to various non-single-family housing as the land use "environment" variable. Thus, he implicitly defines the "neighborhood" to be the entire metropolitan area. The results of this study indicate that the median value of owner-occupied single-family housing is significantly affected by the amount of non-single-family housing within the 40 suburbs. Moreover, multiunit structures alone are shown to be a source of negative spillovers for nearby single-unit family structures.

In perhaps the best study to date, Lafferty and Frech (1978) extended Stull's work using more detailed land use data in order to separate the definition of "neighborhood" into two influences that more accurately reflect the effect of spillovers. Basically, the data permit determining the metropolitanwide effects of land use and the effect of the dispersion of land uses within the metropolitan area. For example, they examine the effect of the geographical location of nonsingle housing uses on single-family housing. Their main finding is "that increases in non-single family land uses in a town raise property values if suitably concentrated. But, increasing the dispersion of a fixed amount of these land uses reduces property values" (Lafferty and Frech 1978: 382). More recently, Crone's (1983) empirical results indicate that zoning for multifamily structures has proved to have a negative effect on the value of nearby single-unit family property.

The results of the empirical studies that attempt to estimate the effect of negative spillovers on the value of single-family housing appear fairly conclusive. Using realistic definitions of what constitutes a neighborhood, non-single-family land uses do create negative spillovers. It has also been shown that a certain amount of commercial activity in proximity to residential neighborhoods is preferred by single-family residents.[2] Nevertheless, in fairness to the authors of those studies in which evidence of negative spillovers is found, without exception, each study concludes with the caveat that zoning may not be the best solution to the problem. The exclusionary aspect of zoning remains suspect in each case.

There is also a public policy debate over whether or not subsidized housing affects the values of adjacent nonsubsidized housing. Here, again, the empirical results conform to intuitive expectations. In the construction of public housing in deteriorated neighborhoods, results suggest that the subsidized housing generally produces neighborhood upgrading. Also, the projects have little net effect in the higher rent areas, although the higher rent areas are not adjacent to the subsidized housing (DeSalvo 1974; Nourse 1963). Moreover, in areas in which the income level of occupants of the subsidized housing is comparable to the income levels of adjacent property owners, the subsidized housing has no effect on the values of adjacent properties (Schafer 1972). However, when there is a significant differential between the income levels of the occupants of subsidized housing and the residents of adjacent property, there is "strong statistical evidence that subsidized housing had an adverse effect on the values of adjacent nonsubsidized housing" (Guy, Hyson, and Ruth 1985: 386).

It should be apparent that the negative effect of multiunit housing on the value of single-unit family housing does not necessarily mean that efficient land use requires separation of these two types of residential uses by some form of land regulation. For example, while Crone (1983) found evidence that multiunit family structures proved to have a negative effect on the value of nearby property, the effect on total land prices owing to mixing the two was not significantly different from zero. Therefore, economic efficiency does not require separation of these two uses of land by zoning.

There is, however, an obvious equity issue involved. In the United States, the predominant use of zoning has been to protect the environment of single-unit family residences, a form of protection that the Supreme Court found justifiable in 1926 and reaffirmed in 1974.[3] Since, in a dynamic economy, an individual home owner may suffer a loss with the introduction of multifamily units into a neighborhood, the protection from such a loss may be sufficient justification for the separation of residential land uses through regulation. In addition, it may also be true that the negative effect of industrial and commercial land uses on residential land use has already been minimized through the widespread use of zoning ordinances.[4]

Here it should be pointed out that not only is efficiency in land use difficult to determine, but it is difficult to apply when costs and benefits are subjective or immeasurable. Nevertheless, it will become apparent that many communities do attempt to implement land use policies in an effort to obtain optimal land use. The efficiency argument is addressed later in this chapter.

A DESCRIPTION OF A DYNAMIC THEORETICAL MODEL OF OPTIMAL LAND USE

In an excellent theoretical analysis, Henderson (1980) demonstrates that residential land use accomplished by developers in a competitive market is not only Pareto optimal, but that it is comparable to the use of land that would obtain if the land were owned and developed collectively by members of the community. Henderson's analysis of a dynamic model begins with the results of static stratification models (Tiebout 1956; B. Ellickson 1971; McGuire 1974; and Hamilton 1975a). Basically, these models establish that residents of a metropolitan area will stratify into fiscally independent communities where the residents are relatively homogeneous in tastes and wealth. That is, residents will settle in communities that provide a given level of services consistent with their tastes and wealth.

A major virtue of the model is that it is a dynamic model, hence, it is more applicable to the realities of land use decision making. Assume residents with similar tastes and wealth form a community in time period one in order jointly to consume public services. In time period two, as a consequence of population growth, additional residents join the community, yielding some positive (or at least nonnegative) benefits to either the developer or the residents or both. Next assume that the developer owns all of the land within a community (political entity) and that there is competition among developers. This assumption is somewhat unrealistic since it implies that the number of communities is large enough to create a competitive market. Nevertheless, at this stage it is necessary to retain this assumption. Each developer, therefore, is competing for growth among the market of residents. In addition, since the level of services is initially given and will continue in time period two, members of the community are aware of the real estate taxes necessary to provide the level of services in both time periods one and two.

With the level of services given, and so long as competition exists among communities, it can be demonstrated that for Pareto optimality to be obtained, the developer must initially establish lot sizes and prices for time period one and lot sizes for time period two. The developer is thus free to charge whatever he can for lots in period two. However, residents in time period one must know what the lot size in time period two will be in order to determine how much they should pay for a lot in time period one. It is this knowledge that permits time period one residents to achieve their highest level of utility in Henderson's analysis. Smaller lots in time period two than in period one will cause an increase in taxes in period two in order to maintain the same service level. With larger lots in time period two, the reverse would occur.

Without a binding agreement, once into period two, a two-party bargaining situation can occur in which the participants can alter lot size and service level in period two. It is this situation that gives rise to the major criticism of zoning. According to White (1975b), members of the community want to zone for large lots in period two in order to maximize taxes paid by period two entrants and to reduce the number of period two entrants in order to minimize public service expenditure. Alternatively, following Edelson (1975), developers desire to sell small lots in period two in order to maximize their remaining profits.

Under the assumption that consumers are risk averse, they will always choose a community in which the developer offers a binding agreement. Since competition prevails in the market for communities, developers are forced either to offer a binding contract or to exit. Thus, consumers are able to maximize their utility. Moreover, if consumers are able to change the rules in time period two, the developer also maximizes returns by forming a binding contract.

Note that it does not matter whether developers set large lots in time period one and small lots in time period two or any other combination. So long as there is a binding agreement, in time period one the consumer can determine what price to pay for a lot, given that the level of services and, therefore, tax rates are known. Consequently, the consumer can reach the highest utility level.

Henderson further illustrates that while it is possible for period two bargaining to yield Pareto efficient levels of period two variables, it is an inferior solution because it creates uncertainty. As a consequence, "initial residents can find a binding contract that eliminates uncertainty and guarantees them their best alternative utility level" (1980: 899). The theoretical model thus demonstrates that not only do both the developer and residents prefer a contractual situation, but the solution will be Pareto optimal.

The theoretical structures pose two problems. First, they do not concern the equity issue. However, this will be discussed later. Second, Henderson's model, which is most important for this study, has two assumptions that do not conform to contemporary institutional structures. Namely, he assumes that there are a sufficient number of communities to produce a competitive market and that the developer-community is the same—that is, each developer owns all of the land in each community. Recall that a competitive number of landlord-developers was necessary for both the developer and the consumer to reach their highest utility level. Neither of those assumptions conforms to reality in contemporary land use. Yet both assumptions are a prerequisite to the formation of a binding contract.

It is realistic, though, to assume that there is competition among developers. As a consequence, following Henderson's analysis, each developer will be forced by the market to form a binding contract with residents between time period one and time period two for each particular land parcel. These parcels are subdivisions or neighborhoods. With the development of each parcel of land, most communities require the developer to provide some form of plan for the development of the entire parcel. In some cases the entire parcel may be platted, that is, each lot, and what is to be developed on each lot within the parcel, is designated.

These may vary widely. They may include only single-unit family housing, combinations of single-unit, multiunit, and cluster housing, or only high-density multiunit housing. What they include, to a large extent, depends upon the developers' perception of the local market for housing. Most prospective purchasers of lots or housing within a single development are, therefore, aware of the environment of the development upon completion. Hence, a binding contract is formed between the developer and residents in time period one for time period two for each particular parcel. Thus, Henderson's theoretical model does have realistic application.

There may be occasions, however, when residents in time period one are not able to form a contract with the landlord-developer for time period two for a particular parcel of land. Some parcels may be relatively large and the build-out period long enough that the developer does not know the lot size or density of development that the market demands prior to build out. There is, however, a way in which a quasi contract can be formed between the two parties in these situations. This form of contract will be discussed later.

Because there is competition among developers, a binding contract cannot be formed between the residents of one parcel of land and the developer of other parcels. Yet this agreement is necessary if the residents of each parcel and each developer are to reach the highest level of utility. In effect, the residents in any particular parcel not only need to have knowledge of the way in which their parcel will be developed, but they also must have knowledge of the type of development that will occur on adjacent parcels or on parcels within a geographic area that can affect the land value of their specific lot. Lacking this knowledge, they are not in a position to determine precisely the value of each lot within any parcel; hence, they are not able to obtain their highest level of utility. Moreover, without any form of land use restrictions, the chances of developers earning an economic rent at the expense of existing land uses would increase. For example, the development of a particularly attractive land parcel, such as one with large-lot single-unit family housing, would clearly generate an economic rent to the landowner of an adjacent parcel if the parcel were developed in apartment housing. The apartments, in turn, would lower the value of the single-unit family housing. In order to reach Pareto optimality, as Henderson's model demonstrates, it becomes apparent that residents must be able to form a contract with owners of adjacent land parcels, and perhaps even the entire community, between time period one and time period two.

If consumers are to maximize utility, theoretical economic structures stand in sharp contrast with contemporary criticisms of land use policy. The static stratification models demonstrate that consumers with relatively high levels of income will maximize their utility by residing in communities with relatively high service levels, while consumers with relatively low levels of income maximize their utility by residing in communities with lower levels of public services. The same solution will obviously exist in the dynamic model. Given income levels and preferences, consumers with higher levels of income will form binding contracts with communities that provide relatively large lots with relatively higher service levels. There is no dilemma or quarrel with the models. The models produce efficient solutions. Also, the models clearly demonstrate that exclusion will occur in a private market, if by exclusion one means that lower income families will not live in communities with relatively high service levels.

It is apparent, therefore, that the assumptions of Henderson's dynamic model do not conform to reality. The assumption that there are a competitive number of communities with all of the land within each community owned by a single landlord-developer does not exist. Moreover, since there are a competitive number of developers within most communities combined with a large number of residents, the transaction costs of negotiation between the two groups prohibits the voluntary formation of a binding contract between time period one and time period two. It is this type of situation that generates the need for public intervention. The necessity for a public good results from the transaction costs of negotiation between the two groups. In addition, in this situation, a part of one group, the landlord-developers in time period two, may not exist in time period one, which precludes the formation of contract.

Administrative law does, however, provide a way in which the residents in time period one can form a contract for time period two. It is this link between Pareto optimal land use in Henderson's theoretical model and administrative law that provides the rationale for the land use model presented later.

THE FORMATION OF A QUASI-CONTRACTUAL ARRANGEMENT IN A DYNAMIC MODEL

Because landlord-developers do not own all of the land within a community and entry into the landlord-developer market can occur in time period two, a contract, in its pure sense, cannot be formed between residents in time period one and landlord-developers in time period two. However, as Henderson's theoretical model demonstrates, a contract is necessary if both residents and landlord-developers are to attain their highest utility level. This section provides the framework by which a quasi-contractual arrangement can be formed for two time periods between residents of a community and landlord-developers. This analysis draws heavily on the work of Carol Rose (1984).

The Piecemeal Nature of Land Use Decisions

The analysis begins with the assumption that changes in land use regulation, especially zoning, are piecemeal in nature. That is, zoning changes most often occur on a parcel-by-parcel basis. Because the growth and development of a community evolves through time, the development of land occurs a parcel at a time, that is, a piece of land at a time. By its very nature, the development of land is piecemeal. There may be occasions when a zoning change affecting the entire community is made or when a comprehensive plan is adopted that affects large sectors of the community that would not constitute a piecemeal change. Nevertheless, the comprehensive plan can and should be changed. Moreover, it will be pointed out later that, because most land use changes are piecemeal in nature, zoning should be flexible.

Rose recognizes that much of the criticism of existing land use controls concentrates on the exclusionary argument, but that a much older criticism cuts even deeper. "It is that we need a new jurisprudence [system of laws or science of law] of local land decisions . . . because local governments cannot be trusted to deal fairly or carefully even in land decisions with only local consequences" (1984: 245).

Critics object most to the piecemeal changes in local land regulations, including the actual changing of the way in which parcels of land are zoned or rezoned, the granting of variances to specific zoning ordinances, or the conditional use permit. Yet it is these small adjustments that occupy most of the energies of planning commissions and planning staffs. Each of these changes may alter preexisting regulations governing the use of individual land parcels, or some larger, but finite geographic area of the community. Most may appear small because they have little effect on the entire community; they appear to concern only the individual developer, owners of adjacent properties, or the local government. Others, however, may appear small but may actually affect a significant segment of the community. Moreover, the critics charge that local governments make these piecemeal changes unfairly and carelessly.

Part of the problem is that there is no consensus among state courts, or even among court decisions within a given state, as to how local governments should handle land use decisions. The problem involves the issue of whether local governments should act like a legislative body or like a judiciary (a court) in making land use decisions.

The Role of Local Government in Land Use Decisions: As a Legislative Body or a Judiciary

It is apparent that a local government, because it is limited in size and may be vulnerable to capture by a particular interest, should not always be viewed as a legislature. A major obstacle to fairness in a legislative body is "faction." A faction may impose its will at the expense of other groups. As Madison argued in his celebrated *The Federalist No. 10,* the advantage of the "extended republic" (that is, the nation) is that it is so large that it would contain a variety of interests, and that no one faction would dominate all others. When the group is large, action occurs through persuasion and coalitions of interest groups. Through the shifting of alliances and vote trading, all of the parties can expect satisfaction of at least some of their desires. This compromising then assures fairness in legislation. In addition, the clash of multiple interests prevents hasty and ill-considered decisions and forces legislators to take the time to reflect on the true public welfare. Because of these factors, the courts can trust larger legislatures to make fair and careful decisions in most cases.

Rose argues that it is precisely this justification of a large legislature's decisions that contains the implicit criticism of small-scale government: any legislative body elected from a small or homogeneous constituency may be too easily dominated by a single interest or faction. Small-scale governments may not contain multiple interests sufficient to provide adequate and careful consideration of the public well-being. A local representative council cannot always be trusted to act with the evenhandedness of a larger legislature. By the same token, local governments are not very likely to be restrained by the safeguards of a larger legislature in making specific piecemeal land use decisions. It follows, therefore, that courts should not give local governments' piecemeal land use decisions the same deference they give to measures taken by state legislatures.

Courts and critics thus agree that land use decisions should not be treated as legislative acts. Local governments are not large enough to create the coalition-building process that restricts legislatures in the enactment of general measures that affect public welfare issues. Moreover, it is not difficult to see that an attempt to quasi-judicialize piecemeal land use decisions does not provide a viable solution. Theoretically, if a local government is to act like a court, it would require that localities develop comprehensive plans for future growth and development and that future zoning be consistent with the plan. It has previously been argued, however, that the growth and development of a community is an evolutionary process, hence it is simply not possible to predict what the growth will be. Planners are not clairvoyant and plans should not be laid in concrete. Instead, plans should be sufficiently flexible to accommodate growth. Quasi-judicialization would perpetuate a rigid, unrealistic conception of what planning should be. Hence, piecemeal changes are no more quasi-judicial than they are legislative. As Rose states,

We have arrived, then, at a point where it appears that "piecemeal change" local land decisions defy our normal categorizations, and escape the safeguards built into these categories. Neither "legislative" nor "adjudicative" characterizations encompass the full range of considerations attendant upon these small changes; moreover, neither seems capable of ensuring due consideration and fairness in these decisions (1984: 286).

An Alternative Approach

Here it is argued that it is important that the local government develop a plan for growth and development because, despite its difficulties, it contains two important notions concerning piecemeal changes and why they are so problematic. First, it recognizes that local governments cannot be treated as legislatures whose actions are made legitimate and are safeguarded by multiple interests through the compromises in coalition building. Second, it recognizes that the changes themselves are not so much decided by generally applicable rules as by a need to adjust conflicts between private property development, the interests of neighboring property owners, and the local government. Piecemeal changes, thus, cannot be legitimized in the legislative sense, because the parties do not deal with each other very often. That is, the coalitions are not likely to be formed.

There is, however, an alternative tradition in American political thought that has always stressed the possibility of participation in the political process with the option of leaving to legitimize local authority, that is, citizen's participation, backed by possible departure. Put differently, local government actions may be legitimized by factors that differ from those factors that legitimize government on a larger scale. The factors that legitimize large government—legislative fairness and carefulness—are assured by the shifting coalitions among interest groups, while judicial fairness and carefulness derive from the application of consistent norms through the courts. Yet a different set of factors can make local decision making legitimate. This set of factors includes the ability of the individual to participate in the making of local decisions by having a voice in the decision-making process and the right to exit. This notion is both directly applicable and appropriate in land use decisions.

Moreover, in treating piecemeal changes as being different from general legislative decisions it, in effect, treats them as resolutions of property right disputes. Actually, this brings piecemeal changes in line with the original purpose of land use controls—an effort to forestall nuisances or, at least, to minimize negative spillover effects. This attempt to minimize negative spillovers, however, often creates conflicts between neighboring property owners or between property owners and local government plans and ordinances. These conflicts must be resolved fairly. Yet fairness is not automatic in local government land use decisions, either directly as a legislative decision or in its quasi form in administrative law. Increasingly, however, in modern legal literature, there is a method that suggests negotiation, including mediation, as a dispute-resolving model that is appropriate at the local or sublocal level.

In this sense, however, mediation differs from its usual form. Mediation normally applies to a neutral third-party intervention in negotiations between two parties. In this approach, the role of local government is found in both negotiation and mediation-arbitration. That is, the local government as mediator has the authority to impose a solution. The government hears all interested parties and attempts to reach an acceptable compromise. Moreover, the government has a stake in reaching an accommodation acceptable to all parties. The local government does not want to lose, and more often than not attempts to entice, valuable development. Simultaneously, the local government's ultimate position of authority does make a difference since some mediations fail to reach an acceptable compromise. In these cases, local governments must act authoritatively in the sense that all parties are not satisfied. It is in failed mediation-arbitration, that is, when some party is dissatisfied, that the issues appear in the courts, leaving to the courts the problem of determining the care and fairness of the process. The question then becomes how are the courts to assess the reasonableness of failed mediation-arbitration of a piecemeal change?

Piecemeal Changes as Mediation-Arbitration: The Quasi-Contractual Agreement

Local land use regulations, including piecemeal changes, must meet a number of substantive requirements in federal and state law. They must not violate any constitutional right, particularly those involving the first amendment and due process, and they must comply with state legislative or judicial mandates. For example, in New Jersey there has been an attempt to require municipalities to provide their fair share of low- or moderate-income housing by the courts. A mediation model must strive to assure fairness and due consideration. "In local piecemeal changes, the meaning of fairness and due consideration should arise from the elements that legitimize local government. From the alternative tradition in American political thinking, we may identify these elements as participation and withdrawal" (Rose 1984: 297). The process of implementing piecemeal changes thus includes a concept of due consideration that depends upon participation, a voice in the deliberations of the process that may influence the decision of the local governing body. A concept of fairness is enforced by the possibility of exit. In this analysis, Rose draws heavily on the work of Albert Hirschman in his well-known *Exit, Voice, and Loyalty* (1971).

This process thus attempts to ensure due consideration through hearings from interested parties and by striving for acceptable accommodations. Actually, current enabling statutes and local ordinances require that adjacent property owners be informed of requested zoning changes and that all zoning changes are advertised for a public hearing. Hence, piecemeal changes can proceed only after notice to interested groups and after a public hearing at which all interested parties have a chance to speak, both before the planning commission and before the local governing body. Moreover, courts have taken these requirements seriously.[5]

The courts have little reason to second-guess the actions of local governments in making piecemeal land use decisions as long as the local government has provided ample notice to all interested parties and no objections are raised. When notice is given, and no objections are raised, and local approval of the piecemeal change is granted, the courts have little reason to second-guess local authority. However, there may be circumstances in which lack of objection is not a good indicator of objections to development. Land developments whose effects may not be felt immediately, but may impact future development, may not arouse local objections. Development along or adjacent to future infrastructure implementation is a good illustration. Increasingly, these decisions have been made at the local level by reference to preexisting plans and environmental or economic impact studies. Although the requirement of environmental and economic impact studies may be criticized as extending local decision making too far, they make more sense where the procedures for regulatory change derive from a negotiation, mediation-arbitration process.

Even when local governments go through the steps to adequately ensure voice in the process, does this mean that the result is always fair to an individual? Obviously, fairness means different things in different contexts. In a large legislative body, fairness results from coalition-building where all parties may participate in a majority and thus satisfy at least some of their desires. Locally, however, coalition-building assurances are unreliable. In addressing the fairness issue at the local level, Rose suggests that contract analysis of fairness is helpful. Here, there are at least two aspects of fairness: fairness of result and fairness in the bargaining arrangement. It is the latter of the two that is more important in local land use regulations.

The determination of fairness in the bargaining process is simply a matter of ensuring that fairness is defined as protection from surprise. If we understand that land use is an evolutionary process and that regulation is necessary to reduce negative spillover effects, then regulation itself must also be evolutionary, that is, it must continually be subject to change. The manner in which the evolutionary change is relayed to developers and to the members of the community is through local land use decisions, which evolve from the process of negotiation and the pattern established by the community in making piecemeal changes. It is the pattern that undergoes evolutionary change. Therefore, fairness in the process should not produce unexpected changes in land use decisions. Fairness, more than anything else, is a matter of predictability.

In practice, the process may turn out to be more informative than the comprehensive plan that is established at some period in time and then subjected to periodic revisions. If fairness depends upon predictability, then planning is desirable. Yet, if planning documents are vague or general, they may not be a particularly good basis for prediction. Planning in the more modern conception—that is, planning in which there is continuous and careful reevaluation of resources and goals—may enhance predictability in the way that ordinary patterns of change do. In this conception, the goals of planning are manifest in the process of decision making. The pattern of change thus protects citizens from sharp discontinuities in land use control and gives notice to interested parties of the likely outcome of piecemeal changes affecting a given parcel.

There is yet another aspect in using predictability as a basis for fairness. Both a developer or prospective member of a community always has the ability to exit. That is, the developer is not obligated to purchase property that needs a seldom-granted zoning change, nor need a property owner go through the expense of requesting an unlikely zoning change. By the same token, a prospective home owner has the same right of exit if the home owner does not like the way the community is developing. It is the predictability that makes the exit possible.

It is also true that while predictability makes exit possible, the likelihood of exit provides a check on local government. Communities recognize that many forms of growth are desirable and, therefore, in their decision making they do not want to discourage valuable growth. Actually, most communities encourage and seek valuable growth. Moreover, despite the exclusionary argument, exclusion is much more a neighborhood phenomenon than a conscious community decision. Land use changes occur in a climate of regulation, and, if developers are aware of the climate, they can take into consideration private arrangements. It is only the unforeseen governmental action that is unfair.

Opportunity for exit is obviously not perfectly available nor is the opportunity for exit evenly distributed. Outsiders can more easily exit while home owners often participate more readily since psychic investment or lack of resources makes exit difficult. Here, voice overlaps with exit, but voice gives at least some protection where exit is difficult. Nevertheless, so long as exit is possible, predictability can be a meaningful test of fairness for piecemeal land use decisions.

The quasi-contractual arrangement is thus neatly formed. So long as residents and landlord-developers in time period one are able to predict land use within the community in time period two, in effect, they have a quasi contract with the local governing body. It is also apparent that the contract must be formed with the local governing body, that is, it cannot be accomplished as a private contract between two parties. As a consequence, optimal land use requires a combination of regulation and the free market.

AN OPTIMAL LAND USE MODEL

Optimal Land Use

Optimal land use must meet the criteria of allocative efficiency and equity. Efficiency in resource management allows all members of society to be better off in absolute terms, while equity is concerned with the distribution of claims to the use of resources and involves decisions about entitlement. Obviously, changes in the institutions that govern land use will substantially affect the distribution of property rights.

Economic efficiency poses special problems with respect to the analysis of optimal land use. Clearly, land use changes can not be Pareto efficient, because it requires that a change in allocation between parties is superior to another if and only if it makes at least one person better off and no one worse off. In the actual economy, most allocative changes, and especially those caused by the public sector, may cause many people to be much better off while some may be worse off. For example, the implementation of infrastructure, such as roads, sewer, and water, into an undeveloped area will increase the property value of landowners who can utilize the infrastructure. Suppose, however, the new road draws traffic away from existing commercial establishments. Society may be significantly better off as a result of the new road, yet owners of the existing commercial establishments will be net losers. As areas in transition change, for example, from lower to higher levels of density, society may be better off, but some of those who do not want the level of density to change are made worse off. For example, some landowners may prefer no change, which suggests that the psychic value of their land in its current use exceeds the increased monetary value that may accompany higher levels of density.

An additional problem exists because the definition of land use efficiency varies among members of society. Efficient land use to landlord-developers may be utilizing land to its highest dollar value given that they do not have to pay compensation for creating negative spillovers, while efficient land use to residents may include maintaining the ambience of the neighborhood and the community. The issue also becomes compounded if one party, such as initial suburban residents, claims priority on the grounds that "they were there first."

It thus becomes apparent that the Pareto efficiency approach in land use is difficult, if not impossible, to apply because costs and benefits are subjective or immeasurable. Yet, optimality in land use can occur under the Kaldor-Hicks criterion of efficiency. That is, as long as land use changes generate benefits to society that exceed losses to individuals that do not reflect a pure taking without due compensation, clearly society is better off.

A MODEL FOR LAND USE

Here the usual caveat enters. The existing distribution of property rights has evolved through accepted legal processes, and the equity of the existing distribution depends upon the fairness of the processes. Further, it is assumed that adequate land is available for development, an assumption that is not unrealistic. A large part of the urban development that will occur in the near future will take place in urban areas in the South and the West, in which geographic space does not impose a binding constraint. Moreover, these are geographic areas that tend to encompass relatively few political jurisdictions, thereby substantially reducing the probability of land exhaustion within a given jurisdiction.

A schema for regulating land use can be developed that will approach an optimal solution, given the existing institutional structure for determining land use. Following the format of the comprehensive plan, tracts of land are designated for particular uses. That is, taking into consideration the geographic areas where growth is anticipated to occur, undeveloped tracts of land are designated commercial, industrial, and residential. Obviously, these geographic areas are determined, to a large extent, by existing and planned infrastructure. A major stipulation is that the aggregate size of each type of land use designation be large enough to ensure a competitive land market within each use throughout the planning period. Although the planning period may vary, it should conform to full implementation of the infrastructure planned for that period. As with any plan, it should be subjected to periodic revision.

Conservation districts and agricultural and forest land are also included in the comprehensive plan. Stringent growth controls are normally an inherent aspect of conservation districts and probably a major reason, along with tax advantages, why landowners request certain parcels to be so designated. They usually require relatively large land parcels, perhaps as much as a few hundred acres, and the land is to remain in the conservation district category for a minimum number of years. The local governing body should not be permitted to designate land for a conservation district. The request should originate with the landowner(s). While minimal development for private use should be permitted in the agricultural and forest districts, development for residential subdivisions, commercial uses, and industrial uses should not be permitted.

The plan itself should be relatively rigid in that only evolutionary changes[6] should result in land uses that do not conform to designated uses in the plan. The comprehensive plan thus encourages competition in the supply of land within specified uses but restricts competition among alternative land uses. Relatively rigid adherence to the comprehensive plan accomplishes two purposes. First, because optimal use of land is a primary purpose of land regulation, optimal use of existing and potential infrastructure implementation should be a major goal in guiding the growth and development of the community. Since the purpose of the infrastructure is to permit private-sector growth, and being cognizant that the infrastructure is provided by the public sector, optimal resource allocation subsumes optimal utilization of the infrastructure by the private sector. Therefore, unless there is a high degree of substitutability between competing land uses for comparable infrastructure, optimal land use requires that the comprehensive plan be a stringent guide to the major types of development. In addition, adherence to the comprehensive plan embraces both a major concern that led to the initial adoption of land use regulation and a continuing concern of advocates of regulation. Simply, it is a distrust in the market mechanism for the allocation of land, which is manifest in the negative spillover argument. The main focus of the negative spillover argument reflects a concern over noncompatible land uses among the major categories of use, especially between residential and commercial-industrial. Adherence to a well-designed plan can significantly reduce the negative spillover effects among the major categories of land use.[7]

In contrast with strict adherence to the plan, zoning within each use classification should be flexible. While the regulation of land among competing uses can help produce a more optimal allocation of land, land use within each classification should be determined by the market. That is, within the constraints of public health, safety, welfare, and the availability of infrastructure, the type, form, and density of development should be determined through the mechanism of the free market. Undeveloped parcels of land should not be rezoned for particular types of development prior to the request for the development of any particular parcel.[8] This requirement obviously precludes zoning large tracts of land for particular types of development, such as large-lot single-family development, prior to a perceived demand. As a consequence, given the competition for land parcels within the residential areas, land prices for housing will be determined competitively and development will reflect consumer demand.

It might be argued that such a high degree of flexibility in the zoning process would simply approach the free market solution and, consequently, negate the need for zoning. This, however, is not the case. Henderson demonstrates that Pareto optimality in a dynamic model requires a contract between residents in time period one and landlord-developers in time period two.

In practice, there are two aspects to the contract. The comprehensive plan itself forms the first part of the contract. It designates in time period one the geographic areas for each major category of land use in time period two. Residents and landlord-developers are, therefore, in a position to predict the geographic areas for land use by major category in time period two. Land use regulation that forces compliance with a comprehensive plan segregates non-compatible land uses, thus reducing negative spillover effects. In addition, growth and development in accordance with the plan helps ensure optimal utilization of existing and planned infrastructure.

The second aspect to the contract is Henderson's notion that residents must know the size of lots in time period two if they are to reach their highest level of utility. In reality, residents are seeking a contractual arrangement that will permit them to predict the integrity or ambience of both the neighborhood and the community in time period two. Residents are aware that growth and development will change the character of the community. Any significant growth will change a community's character. Residents in time period one want some assurance that if they move into a neighborhood within a community, as development occurs it will not change the integrity of their neighborhood or the community. This is not to imply that residents are opposed to multiunit family housing or cluster housing of condominiums or town houses. They simply need to know what the community will be like in time period two in order to determine the value of land in time period one. This argument involves the controversy over private and collective property rights, which will be fully developed in chapter 5. It is briefly introduced here simply to add a bit of reality to the reason why residents desire a contract between time period one and two.

The second aspect to the contractual arrangement is fully developed in the preceding section. It is not possible for residents in time period one to enter into a contract with landlord-developers in time period two. It is possible, however, for residents in time period one to have a quasi-contractual arrangement with respect to land use in time period two through a third party, the local governing body. The justification for such an arrangement in administrative law is through voice and exit.

While voice in the process eliminates the element of surprise in making land use decisions, the decisions to change land use policy should contain a high degree of fairness. There is fairness in the process so long as the changes that are made are consistent with the way in which the past development of the community has evolved or that the changes do not deviate inordinately from past development. For example, if a community has developed in predominantly single-unit family residential neighborhoods with lots of one-half to one acre, the community should not be able to change all single-unit family lots to two-acre minimum size. However, if for economic reasons higher net densities such as cluster housing are desired by households, gross densities comparable to past development would not constitute an inordinate change.

Occasionally, however, inordinate changes may be necessary. The recent creation of overlay districts for the watershed area for reservoirs for future water supply is an excellent illustration. In order to prevent pollution of the reservoir, the density of development permitted within the watershed area may be less than current density levels in other areas of the community.

One of the most intriguing features of a land use model based upon a relatively rigid comprehensive plan combined with flexibility in the zoning of land is the ease with which it can be implemented into the existing institutional structure. In reality, the model, with slight variations, is already being used in many communities. It is, in effect, the process of developing land use policy and the process of implementing land use policy described in chapter 2. The major difference between the model and current institutional land use practices at the local level is that all land in most communities is currently zoned for a specific use.

The contract between residents of a particular neighborhood in time period one and landlord-developers in time period two is usually rather easily arranged. Most often, when residents buy into a neighborhood (subdivision or housing development) in time period one, they are aware of what the ambience of the neighborhood will be in time period two. If part of the neighborhood is undeveloped, the landlord-developer may have recorded the plat for the entire development, or will have a master plan of the entire development. The ambience of the neighborhood in time period two is hence easily determined. Master plans are, however, subject to change. In those cases where the entire neighborhood has not been platted and recorded in time period one, the contractual arrangement is the same as the arrangement for the community in time period two.

The quasi-contractual arrangement between the residents of time period one and the ambience of the community in time period two is that of voice and exit. Voice may initially occur between the planning staff and the landlord-developer, then move to a subcommittee of the planning commission, and on to the full planning commission. Voice from interested members of the community usually enters during public hearings before the planning commission and the governing body. It may occasionally enter at the subcommittee level of the commission.

In controversial land use issues, voice may lead to negotiation. Negotiation enters and follows the same sequence as voice. It may begin with the landlord-developer and the planning staff, move through the subcommittee to the commission, and on to the governing body. Negotiation can also begin at any stage. The results of any negotiations can be formalized only at the level of the governing body. It is here that the local governing body becomes the mediator-arbitrator in the process of land use decision making.

There is one problem in voice as part of the quasi-contractual arrangement that has been raised by many commentators. Specifically, it relates to the fact that the process does not permit voice from those who do not presently reside within a community. More specifically, the notion is a part of the exclusionary argument. Those who are excluded might disagree with land use practices of a particular community, yet they have no voice in the process. The dilemma might partly be resolved through federal or state guidelines, but it is probably through the court system that outright exclusionary practices will be resolved.

SUMMARY

In this chapter three aspects of land use decision making have been combined. Henderson's theoretical analysis demonstrates that for both residents and the landlord-developer to reach their highest utility level, a contract between time period one and time period two must be formed. Residents desire a contract that provides two kinds of protection. First, they want protection from direct spillover effects of neighboring properties that includes protection from noncompatible land uses, such as commercial or industrial. Second, residents desire a contract that offers some protection with respect to the way in which the community will grow. That is, recognizing that communities will change, residents increasingly would like to maintain the integrity or ambience of the community.

Optimality also requires that the landlord-developer form a contract with residents between time period one and time period two. Without a contract, residents can change the rules of the game in time period two, thereby reducing the returns to the landlord-developer.

However, because there is competition among landlord-developers and there are many residents, the contract must take the form of a public good. Rose has demonstrated that a contract can be formed, but since we are concerned with a public good, the contract requires regulation by the public sector. The contract formed is one in which land use regulation, including piecemeal changes, meets the substantive requirements in federal and state law. This contract is accomplished through negotiation and mediation-arbitration, which must ensure fairness to both parties, when fairness is defined to be the protection from surprise. The residents of the community have a voice in the process both through the election of local officials and expression during public hearings concerning piecemeal changes, as do landlord-developers. The evolving land use decisions actually become more informative than the comprehensive plan. Fairness in that process, more than anything else, is a matter of predictability. Both parties are thus in a position to predict the outcome of piecemeal land use changes. Moreover, the possibility of exit adds an additional dimension to fairness.

The combination of economic theory and land use jurisprudence leads to an interesting conclusion. In chapter 2, it was demonstrated that this is precisely the process through which land use policy and land use decisions are currently implemented in many communities throughout the nation with minor variations. The protection (the contract) that both residents and landlord-developers seek is inherent in the existing combination of land use regulation and the free market. Residents have the assurance that the integrity of the community is considered in piecemeal changes, and landlord-developers have assurance of the way in which growth can and will occur.

Many land use changes, including rezoning, are noncontroversial. Landlord-developers often request changes in land uses that are consistent with the comprehensive plan and/or the land use policy as viewed by the public sector. These changes are routinely implemented. Although they do lead to longer run changes in the character of the community, even though piecemeal in nature, they simultaneously protect the ambience of the community. By the same token, changes in the comprehensive plan and the planning for and implementation of infrastructure by the public sector are constantly taking place in a manner that will eventually alter the character of the community, yet attempt to retain its integrity.

There are, however, many changes requested by landlord-developers that are not consistent with optimal land use from the viewpoint of the public sector. In many instances, these requests result in compromises in which deals are struck between the landlord-developer and the public sector. The deals can vary significantly. Developers may be required, at their expense, to extend public infrastructure beyond existing locations, such as sewer and water lines; to provide rights-of-way and sometimes to construct transportation accesses, such as turn lanes; to provide open space for recreation areas; and to decrease overall density levels of build-out of the parcel, to name just a few. Moreover, these deals are accomplished without specific guidelines, and they may vary significantly among various land parcels. Nevertheless, they are deals that reflect a compromise between landlord-developers and members of the community through the local governing body.

In this chapter, a model for land use decision making and the implementation of land use decisions is presented. The full justification for the model will be presented in chapter 5. There are several important land use issues that need to be addressed with respect to any land use model. These issues are discussed in chapter 5. However, in order to judge the merits and drawbacks of the model presented in this chapter, this model must be compared with alternative models of land use. During the past few years, several alternative models of land use have been developed. Each of the alternative models is discussed in chapter 4.

NOTES

1. Babcock (1966), Davis (1963), D. Mills (1979), E. S. Mills and Oates (1975), E. S. Mills (1979), Nelson (1977), Siegan (1972), and White (1975a). While this list is not exhaustive, it is important to note that, although the criticism appears universal, the degree to which zoning is criticized varies among authors and according to assumptions, especially with respect to the degree to which a community attempts to exercise monop-

olistic power. More recently, *Resolving the Housing Crisis* (1982) edited by M. Bruce Johnson contains 15 papers, many of which focus on criticisms of zoning.

2. For example, Li and Brown (1980) find that accessibility to commercial establishments dominates the externality imposed on residents. Using Stull's definition of neighborhood, however, a relatively small amount of commercial activity within residential areas creates a convenience to home owners, but beyond 5 percent commercial activity leads to a decline in home owner property values.

3. *Village of Euclid v. Ambler Realty Co.* (1926), and *Village of Belle Terre v. Borass* (1974). For a fuller discussion, see chapter 1.

4. These obviously vary from community to community. My experience suggests that there are two primary categories of requests for changes. One is the request for locating small business establishments on land designated for residential use. Examples include requests to include an automobile parts establishment, a restaurant, a motel, and various types of businesses conducted in the home. Moreover, the location of these uses is often within existing residential areas as well as land designated for residential use. The second predominant category is requests to develop residential areas in locations that are prime commercial or industrial sites, even though there is more than adequate land available for residential development within the community, and inordinate amounts of land have not been designated for commercial or industrial use.

5. See Carol Rose (1984), notes 19–22, p. 249.

6. An evolutionary change is something that cannot be predicted, such as a technological change in transportation or a change in housing structure or design.

7. To those familiar with land use literature, it should be obvious that the development and implementation of a comprehensive plan is not novel. It has been advocated for several years. For example, see Clawson (1971: 345). It has also been advocated by harsh critics of zoning as will become apparent in chapter 6.

8. It should be noted that it is primarily landowners and realtors, not developers, who oppose initiating zoning until a reasonable time prior to development. Developers know the type of development they propose to initiate, and they are often more than willing to work with the public sector in achieving development compatible with existing and planned land use. For example, developers often offer proffers with respect to how the land will be used, which, in effect, eliminates other uses of the land. Realtors, on the other hand, do not like the designation of land for specific uses such as with proffers, since it limits the speculative aspect of the land parcel, including the speculative aspect in zoning changes, and alternative uses of the land if the original development fails. In the latter case, however, landowners can just as easily request a change in the original proffers. This form of zoning is not, therefore, restrictive.

4
Alternative Forms of Land Use

A model of land use regulation combined with the free market was presented in chapter 3. It has been suggested that not only does the model conform to reality, but when combined with the legal rationale, it provides a framework for a realistic approach to optimal land use in suburban communities. Land use has been shown to be efficient in the Kaldor-Hicks sense, although some equity issues have been addressed. The issue of equity will be discussed further in chapter 5. However, the model in chapter 3 is just one of several alternatives to how land allocation might occur in a capitalistic society.

The purpose of this chapter is to provide a review or summary of several of the alternative proposals that have been set forth as a means of providing a more efficient and equitable system of land use than the present system. An understanding of the merits and drawbacks to each alternative is a prerequisite to judging the merits, drawbacks, and implications of the model of chapter 3. The reader should be aware that each of the alternatives discussed in this chapter has been proposed primarily as an alternative to zoning, although each recognizes the existence of a comprehensive plan.

There is no particular reason to the order in which each alternative is presented. Following each presentation, a prospectus of the merits and drawbacks is provided.

The discussion begins with Frank Popper's land consumerism movement. Actually, land consumerism is not a true alternative in the same sense that each of the others is. Rather, it is a political means whereby consumer groups, through coalitions with other groups, might jointly influence legislative change that brings about a more optimal use of land. Robert Ellickson's well-known article in which covenants combined with nuisance law and fines are proposed as an alternative to zoning is followed by Robert Nelson's notion of advocating neighborhood collective property rights as an alternative to zoning. The transfer of development rights alternative is presented next. This alternative is not attributed to any one particular author since it appears to have evolved through the contributions of several people. Douglas Kmiec's land use intensity system is followed by the concept of inclusionary zoning. Inclusionary zoning is not proposed as an alternative. Because, however, it has been implemented in some areas, the notion deserves attention and understanding. William Fischel's property rights approach is the last alternative presented. In this approach, he argues that property rights should be viewed as an entitlement, that zoning should be alienable, and that zoning should be explicitly fungible.

There is a common theme or concept that pervades the notions that are offered as pure alternatives to zoning. In one way or another, the market replaces zoning as the means of allocating land use. Each alternative does recognize, however, that some form of regulation is necessary. As the reader will become aware, each alternative, in itself, is found to be lacking as a viable solution to optimal land use. Throughout many of the alternative approaches, the reader will also become aware of several similarities in the reasoning of each alternative and the reasons behind the model presented in chapter 3.

A LAND CONSUMERISM MOVEMENT

Frank Popper (1981) has rightly observed that the opponents of land use regulation, primarily those with ownership interest and their allies in government, can usually exert enough control over centralized bodies, particularly at the state level, to weaken their effectiveness. Since centralized regulation can attain only a portion of its objectives because it must deal with these ownership interests, the land use reform movement appears to be at an impasse. Hence, the nation is not completely ready for land use reform, at least not in the form of centralized control at the state or regional level. While this appears to be a valid interpretation of societal views, recall that in chapter 1 a rather different interpretation of the land use reform movement was presented. There it was suggested that, from a local perspective, the right to private property includes an inherent constitutional right to the protection of owned property.

Yet it is apparent that land use regulation, as it exists, is in need of reform. Moreover, as Popper indicates,

what needs reforming in land use is not any single general problem but rather an array of separate problems. These include the new growth, the economics of rapid development, energy projects, the decline of small scale agriculture, and the deficiencies of zoning. Each problem is different; each is complex in itself; and each relates to others in intricate, perhaps unknowable ways (1981: 217).

Centralized regulation may be a suitable approach for some of these problems, but clearly it cannot solve them all. There are, however, programs that appear politically feasible, and they do not conflict with centralized programs. Popper's solution is land consumerism. He believes the reform movement has been out of touch with the real issues. The movement's true interests appear to revolve around aesthetics rather than the issues that actively concern most Americans. These issues include the community economic issues, energy, housing, and racial issues. However, the movement can break out of this tradition by seeking to represent the interest of consumers of land. Everyone is a consumer of land in various capacities, including owner or renter. The capacities include the tax base, a user of public services that includes the infrastructure, and a consumer of other public and private services. Hence, all economic units, households, corporate and noncorporate enterprises, and government are consumers of land.

As consumers they have many common characteristics. They want land that is as cheap as possible, and they want land taxes to be as low as possible. Yet they simultaneously want the land to yield a fair return on investment, both in financial terms and in terms of the emotional value attached to the living environment. They want minimal negative spillovers from other land uses, and they want public decisions with respect to land use to be equitable. The interest of land consumers is thus primarily economic.

The argument is that these universal interests have rarely received governmental attention. Land use regulatory bodies have given them sparse attention, development forces have concentrated on their own profits, and the land use reform movement has generally treated it as a dirty little secret. Because the economic interests of land consumers have not played a part in public decisions concerning land use, land consumers as a group have suffered economic losses through higher land prices, construction costs, taxes, and utility bills.

Better land use would thus be a way of saving money and protecting property investments. It could be a means of both producing and conserving energy. It could also be a measure to encourage economic growth, to lower inflation, to provide lower priced housing, to revitalize the inner city, and to reduce racial and economic inequality. Better land use could foster reductions in sprawl and highway construction, lead to less wasteful building practices, and generate migration back to the central city—many of the things that the reform movement was unable to attain through centralized regulation.

Such a movement should join forces with several groups that share goals for better land use. For example, keeping housing as affordable as possible and the suburbs as accessible as possible are goals that many liberal consumer protection, low-income, minority, fair housing, tenant, and good-government groups espouse. The goals of expanding the low- and middle-income housing markets, keeping taxes and land prices low, and providing cheaper and more efficient government services are virtues shared by conservative developers, businesspeople, construction and other unions, home owners, farmers, local governments, and taxpayer groups. The notion is that there are many common elements in the arguments of both conservatives and liberals. With many common characteristics, land consumer coalitions could form that could free the movement from the inevitably losing position of challenging the strong ownership position. These coalitions would allow the movement to exploit differences between ownership interests and, thereby, induce some of them to work within it to promote land-consumer ends.

For example, the land-consumer approach would allow the movement to take advantage of differences within particular ownership interests. The issue of the price of housing presents obvious political opportunities. Developers of luxury homes will not be greatly concerned over housing prices, but the more numerous developers of middle-income housing, along with the construction industry, desire to keep housing prices within the range of these households. First-time purchasers of new homes will obviously welcome such a coalition. While those in the upper income groups and owners of large land parcels may be opposed, they will be a minority. Hence, those groups in favor of land consumerism will outnumber the opposition presenting a politically favorable situation in contrast with that of the land use reform movement.

To introduce this perspective into the public policy arena, land-consumer coalitions might press for public and private agencies to represent their interests at both the state and local levels. They might work for appointments to state land use agencies for members that represent their interest. They might also support attempts to simplify bureaucratic procedures at both the state and local levels. These groups could attempt to determine which development regulations lead to such unproductive, environmentally unnecessary costs and strive to alter or eliminate them. Land consumerism is thus not incompatible with environmentalists' principles. Environmentalism can succeed only by addressing the public's concerns: land prices, housing availability, tax rates, public service levels, utility bills, and other prices. It can achieve little by calling for pollution controls and aesthetic improvements and then suggesting that these amenities are too trivial or demeaning to discuss.

In brief summary, this reflects the land consumerism reform movement as suggested by Frank Popper.

Prospectus

As with most alternatives to zoning as a means of land use regulation, it can be argued that land consumerism does have merit. In one sense, it does seem rather improbable that the coalitions necessary to generate a real reform movement will be able to combine forces in a manner that will be politically effective. For example, the philosophy of land developers reflects the land ownership interest. Moreover, the philosophy of many contractors tends to be consistent with the developer interest, although, logically, their philosophy should be consistent with consumer interest. Viewed from a different perspective, however, it may well be that society is already in the midst of implementing land uses that might be called land reform. There are several common elements in the existing implementation of land use policy in many communities and land consumerism.

As communities initially adopted zoning as a means of land use regulation—which was briefly discussed in chapter 1—it was necessary that they simultaneously establish planning commissions, which usually consisted of members of the community appointed by local elected officials. Understandably, the elected officials often appointed those persons who they felt were most knowledgeable in land use issues. As a consequence, planning commissions were often dominated by developers, realtors, and members of the construction industry, and their interest pervaded the philosophy of development at the local level. Moreover, the administrative staff, who were responsible for adopting the initial zoning ordinances and presenting staff reports to the commissions and the elected bodies, were, for the most part, not well trained in the implementation of zoning ordinances and the implications of zoning changes. During the recession of the 1930s, economic growth and its ramifications were not an issue—the lack of it was. It was not until the rapid growth era of the 1950s and its aftermath that society found a need for concern about growth.

In addition to the awareness and concern over environmental issues and the fiscal consequences of rapid growth and development, two other forces began to emerge in the 1960s. One, the concern by members of society became manifest at the local level. The attitude of local elected officials reflected society's view as did their appointments to local planning commissions or zoning boards. Second, it was during the decade of the 60s that planning as an academic discipline went through a period of significant growth and change. The increased enrollments in institutions offering a master's degree in planning predominantly resulted from an increased demand by the public sector and to some extent the private sector. Demand grew for administrative staff positions to develop and implement comprehensive plans and local land use ordinances. Heretofore, many localities had few, if any, professionally trained persons in staff positions. Planners were not only responsible for the administrative role but, during the early stages, they at least attempted to educate local officials on the virtues and means of planning for growth.

Through these changes at the local level, local governments increasingly reflect society's views toward land use. Planning commissions of the 1970s and 1980s tend to reflect the full spectrum of land use attitudes, ranging from the most conservative property rights' notions of owners of large tracts of land, developers, and realtors to those who advocate a managed growth philosophy and the concern of environmentalists. Especially in suburban communities, the more urbanized the community becomes, the more the power changes toward managed growth. Put slightly differently, the more urban the environment, the more society becomes concerned over negative spillover effects.

Land consumerism, therefore, may be working. For example, as zoning ordinances are changed and updated, the developer interest on planning commissions is able to exercise a significant impact in enhancing the viability of ordinances that impose unnecessary economic requirements on development. Also, managed growth advocates attempt to set the tone for gross density requirements. In this respect, it is interesting to note that planning commissions often take the leadership role in the implementation of innovative development. In many communities, changes in zoning requirements have been introduced in order to entice developers to utilize Planned Unit Developments and cluster housing.

Land consumerism may be working but, if it is, the way in which it is working is not quite as Popper suggests. It is clearly not through coalitions of various groups influencing state legislatures. If it is working, it is at the local level of government.

COVENANTS, NUISANCE RULES, AND FINES

One of the first specific alternatives to zoning as a means of land use regulation has been articulated by Robert Ellickson (1973a). Ellickson is a harsh critic of zoning and contends that the prevalent system of land use control has both major criticisms and fundamental weaknesses. The basic criticism is that zoning is less efficient and less equitable than available alternatives. Further, zoning is too rigid, its administrative costs are too expensive, and it works to the detriment of the poor, the near poor, racial minorities, and renters.

Zoning administrators either ban or restrict the location of undesirable uses, and where noxious uses are permitted, they are usually placed in locations where adjacent activities are not particularly vulnerable to the noxious use. This is evident in most comprehensive plans of communities throughout the nation. These decisions thus obviously reduce the nuisance cost that would occur if land uses were distributed randomly. Yet, land uses that would occur in lieu of zoning may also be better than random. Industrial uses seek good transportation access and do not prefer to locate near residential land uses. Retail and commercial uses tend to cluster in areas where they have economic advantages from linkages as well as access to consumer markets. Thus, even if a zoning system is more efficient than random land use, it does not necessarily follow that it reduces nuisance costs more than the market mechanism. Moreover, zoning does not guarantee that nuisance costs are either eliminated or internalized. Since about three-quarters of all rezoning applications are approved, it is quite likely that many landowners will suffer losses while others are permitted to use the land without bearing its full social costs. Where zoning is in such a state of flux, Ellickson believes a landowner could receive better protection in other ways.

A major criticism, however, is not that zoning ordinances will fail to eliminate nuisance costs but that the drafters of zoning ordinances will try to eliminate all of them. Basically, he believes planners will impose such restrictive controls that they will create inefficiently high prevention costs. Examples include minimum lot sizes larger than consumers desire, which increases infrastructure costs, and the adoption of ordinances designed to promote the interest of single-family home owners who generally do not advocate a progrowth philosophy. While public expenditure for the administration of zoning is not inordinate, Ellickson does argue that private administrative costs are substantial. These costs are incurred in the process of obtaining a zoning change that may necessitate lawyer fees, consultant fees, or even a public relations campaign.

With respect to the equity issue, as usually implemented, Ellickson believes zoning is inequitable. When zoning increases the value of a land parcel, the owner incurs a windfall gain and is not required to share the wealth. Conversely, when zoning reduces property values, the owner is not compensated unless he or she can obtain a judicial decision that the ordinance constitutes an unconstitutional "taking."

Ellickson believes there are three fundamental weaknesses of the institution of zoning. First is the exclusive reliance on mandatory public standards. Zoning is thus an example of what has been termed a specific deterrence. Such a system can impair the efficiency of resource allocation when it requires compliance with a standard, even though the prevention costs involved in compliance exceed the reduction in the nuisance costs. Second, the initial adoption of a zoning ordinance will simply mirror existing land uses and, therefore, is not capable of dealing with existing land use problems. Moreover, zoning issues tend to concentrate on prospective development proposals and do not address land use problems in general. The third weakness stems from the variability in the way in which identical parcels of land may be zoned and the frequency with which the zoning of land parcels can change. This nonuniform regulation leads to inequity in the system.

In order to eliminate these inherent shortcomings of zoning in the allocation of land, Ellickson addresses the fundamental issues that underlie land use conflicts: the proper distribution of rights among landowners and a system for their enforcement. His alternative land use system relies on a system of covenants and nuisance law doctrine.

A covenant is simply a contract between landowners within a neighborhood, and they can work well in new neighborhoods. A developer will draft a covenant that will bind households who move into the neighborhood or subdivision, and market forces will prompt the drafting of efficient ones. Covenants may cover a variety of things from only single-unit family housing with minimum floor space, to exterior walls, to no visible trailers, boats, or even clotheslines. But neighbors may decide to negotiate for a lesser set of rights than the public may impose through zoning. For example, some neighborhoods may permit the renting of rooms or private businesses in the home. The basic argument in favor of covenants is that through covenants arbitrariness could be reduced by shifting power from the local government to neighbors. In addition, it is argued that covenants reduce administrative costs.

Covenants are specific for each parcel of land. While the developer establishes the initial set of covenants, at some stage of development the control or implementation of the covenants can convert to what are normally referred to as home owners' associations. These are commonplace in many existing neighborhoods, especially in the control and maintenance of recreation areas.

Covenants can obviously be very restrictive and can be used as a device to exclude lower income groups, as recognized by Ellickson. Yet this presents no problem to Ellickson. Any member of an excluded economic class can always potentially have an increase in income, hence economic exclusion is not permanent. Moreover, the external costs imposed upon low-income groups are minor because restrictive covenants will apply to only small portions of land within any community for only a few decades. Because covenants will change as the people within any neighborhood change, that is, as the neighborhood in effect changes through time, Ellickson believes that zoning is more effective than restrictive covenants in achieving class exclusion.

Ellickson argues that we should therefore substitute covenants for zoning and return to using nuisance law, as was used much more prior to zoning. There are four possible remedies in nuisance cases: (1) the plaintiff is entitled to enjoin the defendants nuisance (2) the plaintiff is entitled to damages (3) the plaintiff can neither enjoin nor get damages, and (4) the plaintiff can enjoin but only after compensating the defendant. Ellickson believes that nuisance laws would work better, in general, if the plaintiff is only entitled to remedies 2 and 4. That is, the plaintiff is only entitled to damages and can enjoin only after compensating the defendant. Ellickson believes that the major danger of injunctive relief is that it often exceeds the gain to the plaintiff. So long as the plaintiff is only entitled to damages, this internalizes the nuisance, and, if he must compensate the defendant if an injunction is issued, this discourages the plaintiff from seeking an inefficient injunction.

There are still many problems with respect to land use efficiency and equity that would arise. For example, some neighbors will always be hypersensitive to what others do; but this could be handled on a geographic or local basis. Take a case in which ornamental cedar trees are a host for a disease that is highly infectious to a neighbor's apple trees. If the case had occurred in Nevada where apple trees are rare, it would have been a case of hypersensitivity. But had it occurred in Virginia where growing apples is a large business, it would not constitute hypersensitivity (Samuels 1971).

The combination of covenants with nuisance law does pose the possibility of creating high administrative costs. To remedy this Ellickson suggests the creation of nuisance boards for each metropolitan area and granting them primary jurisdiction over nuisance cases. Each board would use its power to (1) publish regulations stating specifically which land use activities are considered unneighborly by that community at that time, (2) identify hypersensitive uses, (3) establish threshold levels of "substantial harm," and (4) determine schedules of bonus payments for common misuses.

There are other things the community would still have to deal with, especially those things where property ownership is not involved, such as pollution.

Prospectus

Ellickson recognizes that his proposal appears rather drastic. There are several drawbacks to a system of covenants as an alternative to regulation combined with the market. First, it would be virtually impossible to get the members of any neighborhood that is already established, but does not have a set of covenants, to agree on a particular set of covenants. This problem obviously imposes a formidable obstacle to implementing a system of covenants for all neighborhoods. A second practical objection is the difficulty in changing the rules as the result of unexpected conditions. For whatever reason, a desire by some members of a neighborhood to alter a covenant would require the consent of all members of the neighborhood, since covenants are attached to the land. A change in a covenant, therefore, would be just as difficult to accomplish as getting all members of an established neighborhood to agree on any set of rules. As previously mentioned, both of these problems might be overcome by establishing a residential private government, which does not require unanimity, as an alternative to covenants.

Two additional practical problems exist with a system of covenants. One is that covenants are normally enforced by private individuals, which tends to be expensive since the costs are not spread among all of those who might benefit from upholding the covenant. In addition, the enforcement of a covenant by an individual tends to create bad feelings among members within the neighborhood. As a consequence, covenants are often not enforced.

Because covenants are perhaps the most often proposed alternative offered by commentators critical of zoning, it will be useful to understand how well they have worked in Houston, the only large city that does not have zoning. Although Bernard Siegan's (1972) comparisons of Houston's land use with other cities was published 15 years ago, it remains an excellent contribution with many current applications to a study of land use policy. Restrictive covenants vary significantly from zoning in some important ways: it is unlikely that they will affect areas as large as those affected by zoning; they are binding for a period of time specified by their terms; and the state has little discretion in their creation and enforcement. For these reasons, it is argued that they function with far less exclusionary effects than zoning (Siegan 1972: 77).

No two cities are alike. Consequently, it is not possible to make an exact comparison of Houston with another city that has adopted and grown with zoning. Siegan's comparisons are, however, objective and not unexpected, as will become apparent.

Economic forces will cause major categories of land use separation even without zoning. Commercial, industrial, and residential land uses will tend to locate in certain areas. Even within residential sectors, apartment housing will concentrate in some areas and not others, just as segregation among light, medium, and heavy industrial uses will occur. Different types of productive activities require different geographic locations, which often depend upon the location of infrastructure and proximity to markets for certain types of commercial uses. When separation of different productive activities is vital to maximizing utility for household, commercial, and industrial uses and when the market does not guarantee that separation will occur, property owners will enter into agreements to provide such protection. This protection is accomplished through restrictive covenants for residential neighborhoods and can be accomplished between residential neighborhoods and adjoining commercial property. Industrial subdivisions also often enter into covenant agreements.

When covenants expire, land use is most often determined by economic pressures. Commercial, light industrial, and apartment uses begin to occur along major roads where single-unit housing once existed. As the demand for multiunit family housing increases, it will occur in nonrestricted interior areas as well, but it does not extend to all sections of the city.

Siegan suggests that more land along major transportation routes in Houston is used for commercial and multifamily purposes than would have occurred if zoning existed. Further, he believes zoning restricts the supply of some uses and may impede innovation. He does suggest, however, that in major cities, which contain diverse life-styles, zoning probably has responded by accommodating most consumer demands, although he does not believe zoning has worked well in the more homogeneous suburbs.

One conclusion is Siegan believes that if Houston had adopted zoning in 1962 (a vote to adopt zoning was turned down by the citizens of Houston), it would have resulted in higher rents and fewer apartments to the extent that some tenants would have been priced out of the new apartment market. His analysis does suggest that the values of new and existing single-unit family housing is no different in Houston and cities with zoning.

Despite minor problems involving land use in Houston, such as the unsightly billboards and a problem with the supply of groundwater, Siegan's analysis suggests that, without zoning, Houston is not unlike many zoned cities. Two aspects of land use in Houston's history have yet to be discussed, however, one of which is crucial to any land use policy. As Siegan points out, although Houston has never adopted zoning, it has had subdivision controls, a minimum housing ordinance, a building code, and traffic ordinances since 1940. These controls are similar to those considered common to many cities. Moreover, as much as three-fourths of the developed area has been subject to them. Since 1940, Houston also has had a city planning department that functions in ways similar to planning departments in most cities. Because Houston grew with the automobile, private development probably occurred more in accordance with access to infrastructure. Consequently, to the extent that planning did occur, especially with respect to infrastructure location, it may have played a more important role in land use policy than in older cities. As will be brought out later, planning to accommodate growth is a crucial element in providing for optimal land use and in reducing land use conflicts.

In addition, Houston has had a City Planning Commission, which must approve all land subdivisions that contain some controls found in zoning ordinances. While Houston's regulations may be modest compared with many zoned cities, some regulations do exist. For example, minimum lot sizes and setbacks for residential and commercial uses are part of the rules for land subdivision. As Siegan (1972: 75) states: "In the absence of zoning, municipalities will adopt specific ordinances to alleviate specific land use problems."

It should also be noted that the City of Houston enforces private covenants. Such a practice is rare, but it might become a necessity without zoning.

As previously stated, covenants can and do work well in certain situations. As a complete substitute for land regulation, they will not work well, as illustrated even in Houston. It does seem apparent that one of the reasons they have been successful for the citizens of Houston is that Houston grew with covenants. Moreover, Houston did not overlook planning, an issue that will take on greater significance in chapters 5 and 6.

PRIVATE NEIGHBORHOODS

Robert Nelson (1984) has presented one of the most interesting alternatives to the existing institutional structure of land use in the United States. As previously mentioned, Nelson is an articulate critic of zoning. Yet it is interesting to note how his fundamental reasons for advocating neighborhood collective property rights as an alternative to zoning are consistent with the fundamental rationale behind zoning as a form of land use regulation—a major difference being that zoning lacks some important elements of a property right. Primarily, the transfer of zoning rights cannot be accomplished by direct sale, at least not legally. It is also true that zoning does not grant complete discretion to private owners to control the use of neighborhood property. For example, courts limit the ability of neighborhoods to control fine details of uses, such as those that affect only the aesthetic character of a neighborhood, through zoning.

Nelson views the vigorous neighborhood movement of the 1970s as being remarkable in many ways. Throughout most of this century, many urban professionals have disapproved of the excessive decentralization of local government, and they have lamented the social divisions and lack of policy coordination resulting from this division of responsibility. As a consequence, the individual strategies of metropolitan areas or policies that might apply to an entire metropolitan area are often condemned to frustration because of the sheer number of municipalities that constitute the metropolitan area. While nonlocal governments, agents of outside considered parties, and in some cases the courts sought to break down community distinctions in the interest of a more fully homogeneous and equal society, community interest stood for parochialism and resistance to modern social currents.

Simultaneously, the same logic applies to local municipalities and neighborhoods. Local governments often feel frustrated in attempts to implement local strategies for growth and development because of the sheer number and diversity of neighborhoods and their diverse interests. The diverse interests of various groups such as developers and existing households also enter into the problem.

At this juncture, it is important to be aware of the context in which local communities (political entities) are being discussed compared with neighborhoods. Nelson does not provide a pure definition of neighborhood but it is implicit in his discussion that a neighborhood can range from a subdivision of single-unit family households to a much larger geographic area that incorporates many facets of the living environment. It is possible that the two could be the same, but this environment could only occur in a relatively small community. As communities increase in size, the number of neighborhoods normally increases.

For Nelson, it is the emergence of a neighborhood movement that shows the shifting tides of public opinion. It is the neighborhood that now seems attractive because it offers virtues that may be threatened by modern society—cohesiveness of moral values, close personal ties, mutual trust, permanence, and stability. Early in this century, there may have been a longing for a national community as characterized by the Progressive movement. As a leading Progressive theorist, Herbert Croly, stated: "The promise of American life is to be fulfilled—not merely by a maxim of economic freedom but by a certain measure of discipline; not merely . . . by the satisfaction of individual desires, but by a large measure of individual subordination and self-denial" (Nelson 1984: 324). Americans would thus have to subordinate the satisfaction of individual desires to the fulfillment of a national purpose.

There is no longer the confidence today that the nation is capable of fulfilling this role. With a declining sense of national community, interest is instead reviving in local and private forms of community association. A study in 1977 focuses on the role of mediating structures in public policy: church, family, union, and other private institutions that stand between the individual and the state. Mediating structures are seen as performing a critical function because they are agencies for generating and maintaining values in society. Of particular importance is the view that the neighborhood should be seen as a key mediating structure (Berger and Neuhaus 1977: 6 and 8).

In 1979 the National Commission on Neighborhoods (p. 276) concurred on a concept of the neighborhood as a key "mediating structure":

If city, state, and federal governments are to effectively respond to people's needs, and if the natural resource of every person is to be converted into energy for the common good, then healthy neighborhoods are essential. Neighborhoods are human in scale, and they are immediate in people's experience. Since their scale is manageable, they nurture confidence and a sense of control over the environment. Neighborhoods have built-in "coping mechanisms" in the form of churches, voluntary associations, formal and informal networks. The neighborhood is a place where one's physical surroundings become a focus for community and a sense of belonging.

This new role for neighborhoods will thus require a wide diversity of neighborhood types since tastes in neighborhood values and environments are extremely varied. As long as people have a wide latitude to choose among neighborhoods, each individual can join other neighborhood residents with similar values to form an acceptable social environment.

Nelson argues further that

while the neighborhood movement has reflected a discontent with the alienating character of the market, it has also reflected an equally strong discontent with big government and big bureaucracy. Bureaucratic government in its impersonality and unresponsiveness offers little if any improvement on the market, similarly eroding critical social values (1984: 326–327).

The National Commission on Neighborhoods (p. 7) states that "the diversity of neighborhood groups, which may seem to be a weakness, in fact is an important strength." An enhanced neighborhood role will thus create greater sensitivity to the widely varying needs and values of individual neighborhoods.

One of the major criticisms of the growth of big government is that, especially in large cities, it is often the poorest neighborhoods that receive the lowest quality of service delivery. For example, many government programs to aid the poor may turn out to be of greater benefit to the middle class. Neighborhood movements might, therefore, bring a form of suburban government patterns into the central city. Rather than the historical pattern of central city expansion, such as through annexations, the reverse should occur. The suburban pattern of smaller jurisdictions should move into the central city. The respectability of the neighborhood, combined with a long-standing popular support of neighborhoods that now exists in suburban settings, thus offers support for a neighborhood movement within the central city.

The legal legitimacy of the neighborhood would require it to have new collective property rights, similar to those exercised by home owners' associations or condominium owners, that would formally replace zoning. In this manner, a balance could be formed between forces for stability and forces for change. Zoning has worked well in providing stability for many suburban neighborhoods. However, it has long been known that zoning has not worked well in providing flexibility and the possibility of necessary change for optimal land use. This flexibility could be achieved by allowing the right of entry into neighborhoods to become a marketable commodity, subject to normal market forces. This would be a logical accompaniment to the formal recognition of zoning as a private property right.

The implicit assumption of most neighborhoods, as reflected in the design of zoning and other neighborhood institutions, is that they will always remain the same. Local residents are very conservative about their own neighborhoods and are showing increasing signs of becoming just as conservative about adjoining or nearby neighborhoods. Land use, however, is constantly evolving. Consequently, some neighborhoods will always be in a transition stage from one type of use to another. This transition probably becomes most pronounced in residential neighborhoods that, from an optimal land user perspective, evolve from single-unit family housing to a higher level of residential density or from any form of residential housing to commercial or light industrial uses. In addition, there are those cases where infrastructure changes may affect the entire neighborhood or only a portion of the neighborhood. It is also apparent that whatever form of change should occur, all members of the neighborhood are not affected in the same manner. Some may be located so as to derive significant economic benefit from the change, while nearby neighbors may be exposed to a negative spillover. Nothing says the change will be equitable. Moreover, there are always those within any residential area who do not want the area to change, irrespective of obvious advantages to change if optimal land use is to obtain. Zoning, as now implemented, tends to favor the existing land use and, as a consequence, may significantly slow the evolutionary change. It is in this sense that zoning is criticized for being inflexible. When the pressures for a zoning change eventually bring about the change, all landowners within the neighborhood are not equally affected.

Under Nelson's alternative system private property rights would be saleable and the neighborhood, acting as a collective unit, would undertake the transaction(s) and distribute the financial resources. As a result, neighborhood residents jointly make a decision in which an equilibrium is reached with respect to the future use of their neighborhood and the demand for their neighborhood from outside sources. An equilibrium that is reflected in a price for neighborhood entry that is collectively acceptable therefore adequately compensates the members of the neighborhood for disruptions or other negative impacts from new development.

Left to its own devices, the market is a powerful engine for change. When property becomes more valuable in one use than another, market incentives lead to its sale to the user who values it most highly. As long as the transaction is voluntary on both sides, both the buyer and seller benefit. The new buyer receives a property more valuable than alternative uses of the money; the seller, on the other hand, prefers receipts of the payment and the purchasing power it conveys. Currently, neighborhood institutions not only fail to utilize such market virtues, but actively obstruct their functioning (Nelson 1984: 330).

Prospectus

There is little doubt that the full realization of private neighborhoods would constitute a major land reform movement. Private property rights would replace existing zoning. Property rights within the private neighborhood would be divided into individual and collective rights. The collective rights would be confined to common elements of the neighborhood, such as those things affecting the aesthetics of the neighborhood, as well as other types of changes. The decision to substitute private rights for zoning would occur by vote of the neighborhood residents that could require a two-thirds or three-fourths majority, or even a higher proportion, but clearly not absolute unanimity. These new property rights could be exercised through a neighborhood association or some other suitable instrument.

The neighborhood association would then be able to negotiate with potential new users over financial terms of entry into the neighborhood. This could range from small-scale entry of a small office complex or small retail establishment to the sale of the entire neighborhood for a large development. The money would then be distributed to residents according to their relative shareholdings in the neighborhood. In a case in which all residents might not be equally affected, the distribution of shares could be so adjusted.

There would obviously be wide flexibility in the type of private controls exercised over the neighborhood property. Some might prefer no controls or at least minimal controls, particularly those in relatively rural settings. Others might prefer controls to include the fine details of architectural design. The result would clearly be a wide choice in neighborhood types.

There are many virtues to legitimatizing private neighborhoods, and there are existing examples where they work. Some of these will be expressed later. Nelson realizes legitimatizing private neighborhoods would constitute a major land reform. Realistically, a major reform in land use is not likely to occur. Despite the difficulty of implementation, there is an additional problem that Nelson does not address: namely, whether the connotation of neighborhood that he uses is closely akin to a subdivision or some form of housing development, or whether the definition encompasses many facets of our living environment including shopping, institutions of various types, and perhaps even the educational system. Nelson's implicit meaning of neighborhood incorporates what would be, in effect, a small community. This definition poses two problems. First, the formidable task of delineating the neighborhood in this sense manifests the impracticality of the legitimacy of neighborhood as an alternative to the existing institutional structure. Even more difficult would be the implementive task of the distribution of property rights among members of the neighborhood, which would include commercial, industrial, and residential property. In addition, the meaning of neighborhood in its broadest sense, which is implicit in Nelson's view, would not produce significant advantages over zoning as a form of land use regulation. In this sense, the neighborhood simply functions as a small community and the same criticisms expressed against zoning would apply to the way in which the neighborhood uses its property rights in future growth and development.

Despite this major criticism, an implicit meaning of neighborhood (that of a subsidivision or an area with mixed uses but much smaller than a typical community) does have merit, and it could be incorporated into the existing institutional structure of land use. As will be developed later, neighborhood property rights could contribute to optimal land use in two important ways. First, because of the rigidity of zoning in developed property, a major criticism of zoning is that it slows the process of transition of developed property from one type of use to another. Neighborhood property rights would speed the transitional change, especially when the transition is from housing to some other category of land use. Second, neighborhood property rights, again especially in those neighborhoods primarily involving housing, provide a more equitable means of transition.

THE TRANSFER OF DEVELOPMENT RIGHTS

The idea of the transfer of development rights (TDR) has been proposed for some time as an alternative or at least a partial alternative to existing forms of land use. The legal concept underlying TDR is that title to real estate is not a unitary or monolithic right (J. Rose 1974). Instead, it is a right that may be compared to a bundle of individual rights, each of which may be separated from the others and transferred to someone else, thus leaving the original owner with all other rights of ownership. There is actually nothing new in this concept. For example, we have long separated such components of title as mineral rights and mortgage liens. One of the components of this bundle of rights could, therefore, be the right to develop the land. Actually, other than in most agricultural and mining areas, the right to develop is probably the component of greatest value among the rights to ownership. Clearly, however, there is legal precedent for the transfer of just one right, in this case the right to develop, leaving the owner of the land with all other rights.

There are several proposals or programs in existence, although most of them are attempts to achieve one or more specific goals. They have been used as a means to help preserve historical landmarks, to provide or retain open space, to help in the preservation of fragile ecological resources, to encourage moderate- and low-income housing, to regulate the location and timing of local growth, and even to provide the primary system of land use regulation.

A TDR schema as a primary system of land use regulation might work somewhat as follows. The first prerequisite involves specific identification of the uses of land throughout the community. Residential, commercial, industrial, and areas to be preserved such as woodlands, agricultural lands, and environmentally sensitive areas must correspond to the community's master plan. Once these areas are designated the potential development capacity under current zoning must be calculated, converted into development rights (DR), and distributed to property owners in those areas to be preserved. The total number of DRs distributed to landowners in the preserved areas must equal the number of development units that were eliminated. In effect, they represent the development potential of the preserved areas. Each owner receives DRs on the basis of the value of his or her land in relation to the value of land to be preserved, the number being determined by acres, value of land parcels, or some other system.

In order to create a market that will give "value" to the DRs, the local government must designate other districts in which new and higher density development will be permitted if accompanied by DRs. The permitted increase in density in certain areas depends upon the number of DRs issued to landowners in the preserved areas. It is the increase in permitted densities of certain areas over the former zoning that creates the incentive to purchase DRs from DR holders in the preserved areas. The new densities permitted must in fact create the incentive. In any event, it is obvious that planning and zoning are inherent in the implementation of a TDR system.

Because development proposals that conform to the former zoning can be approved with additional DRs, it is possible to have a surplus of DRs. If this were to occur, it would become the responsibility of the local governing body to rezone additional areas in which DRs could be used. It is thus the responsibility of the local governing body to establish and maintain a "fair" market for DRs.

The attractiveness of TDR is clearly the equitable treatment it affords to all landowners. If DRs are assigned in an equitable manner and the market for land (although it is apparent that some direct land use controls will remain) determines the most efficient use for each parcel, landowners who underdevelop are compensated by those who overdevelop and the gains from development are equitably distributed. It is also a method of avoiding the windfalls and wipeouts syndrome. For example, in the implementation of infrastructure by the governments " . . . some property owners are fortuitously visited with enormous increases in land value—they are the windfallers. Meanwhile, and equally by change, other landowners suffer substantial losses in value—they are wiped out by government activity" (Hagman 1975: 265).

Prospectus

In an analysis of the virtues and drawbacks of TDR, realism must prevail in at least one sense. In chapter 3 it was pointed out that if a criterion for public intervention in private land use decisions is economic efficiency, intervention is only warranted when there are imperfections in the urban land market. The most important imperfection results from noncompatible uses of parcels of land that create negative spillover effects. The extent to which the market allocates land efficiently, as a result of spillover effects, then depends upon the extent to which voluntary transactions among land users fail to correct for them. In the case of simple spillovers, the only obstacle to the market resulting in efficient land use is the cost incurred in the transaction. It is also pointed out that in the case where the spillovers take the form of a public good, the free rider problem always exists. In essence, it is argued that negative spillovers would remain after all voluntary efforts to correct them are exhausted. Hence, some form of intervention in the market for land is necessary to approach optimal land use. Moreover, it was further proposed that a combination of planning through the comprehensive plan and zoning as a means of regulation best approaches optimal land use.

This being the case, can a combination of land use regulation and TDR satisfy the efficiency argument and simultaneously provide a more equitable solution in the growth and development of a community? It is apparent that, whereas direct land use controls may reduce some inefficiencies by segregating nonconforming uses of land, they can produce inequitable side effects. By rationing amounts of land within a community to certain uses, direct controls can ration the gains from development or redirect the gains among landowners in an inequitable fashion. Owners of land parcels that differ only in the type of development that can be accomplished on the land, such as multiunit housing as opposed to single-unit family housing, are differentially rewarded. TDR is thus a schema that permits the aggregate level of development within a community to be limited, thereby reducing the negative spillover effects, without differentially distributing the gains from development among landowners.

David Mills (1980) has formally demonstrated the theoretical rationale of the argument. Intuitively, the results are straightforward. The land use regulation policy must not be more or less constraining on competition than the TDR policy. The design of the land use regulation policy, specifically the zoning policy, must be coordinated with TDR.

The obvious way to coordinate the design of such a zoning policy with the TDR policy to assure equalization of gains is to make the redemptive value of DRs so small (or distribute so few) that they enable no more total development than the zoning policy (Mills 1980: 67).

An aggregate TDR policy combined with zoning has two major drawbacks, yet a partial TDR program could substantially contribute to optimal and more equitable land use. The most significant drawback to the aggregate TDR policy combined with regulation is one that has received the least attention. If a combination of the two is to be equitable, it is imperative that the supply and demand for DRs establish an equitable equilibrium price. This equilibrium is not to imply that the price remains constant. In actuality, using the calculus of present value, the exchange price should vary through time as the community develops. However, if the exchange price is to be equitable, it is necessary that the total number of DRs, which are determined in coordination with present and future land use policy, is known. Establishing the total number of DRs explicitly assumes that the future development of the community will be established with the initial issue of DRs. One of two things can be inferred. First, planners are clairvoyant about future growth, that is, they are able to determine future demand for growth in the community. Obviously, planners, whoever they may be, are not clairvoyant. More importantly, however, explicit in this assumption is that at some point in time the full development of the community is determined. That is, in the establishment of the number of DRs to be issued, the future build-out of the community is set. The future level of development is thus established at a given time. This being the case, all of the same criticisms that apply to any form of land use regulation, including the exclusionary argument, apply to an aggregate TDR system. Even if planners do not invoke exclusionary practices for future development, it is apparent that they cannot predict future demand for growth. Hence, the optimal number of DRs cannot be established.

While it may be true that an aggregate TDR system may be able to reduce inequities to landowners, it is apparent that a TDR system cannot eliminate them. More importantly, an aggregate TDR system violates the evolutionary concept of community growth and development. As suggested earlier, given the existing institutional structure of land use regulation, zoning should remain flexible, and there is a means whereby a contract can be formed between landowners in time period one with respect to future growth. It is in this manner that optimal land use can be approached given the uncertainty of future growth and development within a community.

There is one serious problem that is unrelated to objective criticisms in the implementation of a TDR system—a problem that is illustrated well in Strong's (1975) description of the Brandywine experience. The crux of the issue is that the self-interest of current residents is not likely to coincide with the broader interest of planning for those who may be future residents of the community. The implementation of a TDR system requires government intervention in the determination of the dollar value of DRs and takes away the right of landowners whose land is to be preserved. The implementation of a TDR system requires adoption by a vote of local residents. In many communities, current residents do not want to forego the chance to speculate in the market or to seek rezoning of their land for higher returns.

There are, however, obvious merits with TDR in complementing land use regulation. While the competitive market does not allocate land in an efficient manner and local government intervention in the form of direct controls can mitigate this inefficiency, direct controls often carry the unfortunate side effect of redistributing the gains from development among landowners. There are many examples where the preservation of certain land parcels enhances the living environment of a community. Certain land parcels thus produce desirable external benefits when devoted to a particular use that far exceed the value of the land to an individual property owner. Yet the owners are unable to obtain full compensation because of the nonexclusive characteristic of the good. Moreover, when the social value does, in fact, exceed the value to the individual property owner, Pareto optimality can be achieved by an exchange between the public sector and the property owner.

This use of TDRs may be especially applicable in the case of open space and landmark preservation. It may also be true with respect to marginal environmental issues, since there is always a continuum of the degree or extent to which land use controls should be used to protect the environment. Even within an aggregate TDR policy, an equally unsatisfactory result follows from the imposition of a simple TDR policy. That is, within the structure of an aggregate policy, it fails to assure that the right parcels are preserved or left undeveloped.

In the implementation of land use controls, the public sector must always be cognizant of the inequities involved, and many may always exist. For example, positive inequities exist that create windfall gains to "lucky" landowners in the development of infrastructure. The taking issue is, however, very real to certain landowners, especially if land use regulations prevent development for the benefit of the community at the expense of the landowner. TDR thus provides an excellent means of achieving Pareto optimality in land use for particular parcels of land within a community. In addition, the implementation of a piecemeal TDR system does not encounter the formidable practical problems of an aggregate system. It is not necessary to determine a particular number of DRs for a community. Actually, no number of DRs need be determined. The price of development rights for a particular parcel can be easily reached between two players.

A LAND USE INTENSITY SYSTEM

Douglas Kmiec (1983) has presented an alternative land use allocation system for undeveloped land that attempts to remedy what he considers to be shortcomings of the existing system. In essence, he believes the existing system is unfair, inefficient, inflexible, and uncertain and, consequently, has little to recommend it. The alternative seeks to reduce public control by repealing existing zoning and subdivision-enabling legislation as it is applied to undeveloped land. New legislation would limit public control, principally in the areas of development intensity and public improvements, in an attempt to maximize individual freedom and private decision making in the development process.

The alternative system is outlined as follows.

First, all undeveloped land would be reclassified agricultural open space. Second, local legislative bodies and their planning staffs or consultants, together with interested citizens, would then define the land use intensity (LUI) policy for a specified period of time for the undeveloped land within the entire community. Third, the LUI would be expressed in four separate schedules for residential, commercial, industrial, and mixed-use projects.

Each schedule would disclose the maximum density permitted for each type of development (Kmiec 1983: 317–318).

In order to preserve procedural fairness, the legislative body would not specify which land could be developed at any given level of intensity, and the legislative body would not be permitted to allocate any particular portion of the undeveloped land to a particular use. The legislative body could thus indirectly control the growth of the community by setting limits on project density, which it could periodically revise. It could not, however, directly allocate certain parcels or areas of the community for specific use categories.

On the selection of LUI ratings for specific parcels, each landowner would be able to select the intensity desired, up to but not exceeding the maximum allowed under the schedules. Selection is to be accomplished by filing written notice with an administrative body, and, once established, the LUI rating selection would be valid for 180 days. If the rating selection lapses, the landowner, or anyone else with an interest in the property, could not seek the same LUI rating for the same property for one year.

Since the selection of the LUI rating would be determined solely by the landowner, the use of the land, including the development of private improvements, would also be a private decision. In effect, the landowner would be free to develop the parcel for any type of use within the selection of the LUI range. No restrictions on height, bulk, design, parking space, setbacks, or aesthetics would be enforceable by the public sector. The landowner would, however, be subject to the common law of nuisance and certain other public laws, such as building, health, and sanitation codes.

While this alternative system acknowledges that private improvement decisions are best made by the private sector, it also acknowledges that public improvement decisions should be made by the public sector. Thus, the public sector determines the location, quantity, and quality of public improvements in infrastructure. Kmiec believes that under existing law it is unclear what the public sector can require of a landowner in the way of infrastructure of both on-site and off-site public improvements. This alternative system will eliminate this uncertainty with a clear rule. As a condition of development at the selected LUI rating, the landowner shall undertake all on-site and off-site public improvements required by the local public sector so long as the cost of these improvements does not exceed an agreed amount. This agreed amount for public improvements shall be equal to the difference between the fair market value of the property at the owner-selected LUI rating and the fair market value of the property in its agricultural or undeveloped use—that is, the fair market value after selection minus the fair market value before. As Kmiec states, that "... agreed amount equals what Henry George defined as the unearned increment of land value—the value that a given parcel of land has because of adjacent beneficial improvements not attributable to the landowner, be they private or public in origin" (1983: 320).

It is this part of the alternative system that Kmiec finds most attractive. He believes that the existing system of land use allocation is often permeated by a "no growth" attitude because development is viewed as imposing economic costs on local residents and economic benefits on the private landowner. Since this alternative system offers the community the economic value of the unearned increment for public improvement or for the general revenue, it provides an incentive for the community to establish a rational set of LUI ratings that permits a reasonable level of development.

One additional aspect of this alternative is that there may be occasions where the public sector and the landowner may wish to depart from the selected LUI rating for a specific parcel of land. In these cases, the landowner and the public agency must bargain with each other for such a change. For example, higher densities could be permitted if additional public improvements were to be made. These contracts could be as enforceable as any other private arrangement subject to reasonable and necessary impairment to accommodate the police power.

Prospectus

In an analysis of an LUI system as a means of allocating land use, one must bear in mind the philosophical view toward private rights and the full intent of the proposal as developed by its author. Kmiec believes that zoning, and to a lesser extent subdivision regulation, finds its justification in the police power, the criterion for which is to promote the health, safety, morals, and general welfare of the community. Yet, under this general welfare banner, zoning has been used to stabilize property values, to promote homogeneous development, to control competition, to preserve landmarks and to help protect the environment, to refine a community's moral and aesthetic values, to control population density, and to maintain the tax base. Many of these matters should not, or need not, be the subject of land use regulation. His alternative system reflects the belief that it is improper to regulate competition or to impose social and aesthetic preferences and that public regulation distorts, rather than stabilizes, values.

Kmiec further believes that "the neighbor has no greater vested right with regard to his own property interest, and no vested right whatsoever to the rights of an adjacent landowner, unless the adjacent landowner's proposed use would deprive the neighbor of an economically viable use of his land" (p. 344). Thus, if one accepts the argument that neighbors have used zoning to foster their individual interest rather than public policy, Kmiec suggests two alternatives: either expressly authorize neighbor control or expressly eliminate it. As he states, Nelson has chosen the first; he has chosen the second.

Leaving aside for the moment what constitutes private property rights, there are fundamental criticisms of an LUI system of land allocation. In the implementation of the system, it is the members of the community, through the political structure of the locality, who will determine the density of each type of development. As a consequence, permitting the community to determine the level of density will lead to the same dilemma that has provoked much of the criticism surrounding the existing system of land use regulation. In the evolutionary growth of a community from relatively rural to that with a suburban environment, the suburban populace comes to dominate the land use philosophy with respect to growth and development. This suburban philosophy will obviously be reflected in the implementation of infrastructure and in the densities of each type of development, especially housing. An LUI system of land allocation, therefore, will not eliminate two of the major criticisms of the existing system of land use allocation, namely, the exclusionary argument and the provision of low-income housing.

Kmiec does, however, believe the LUI system will eliminate the economic criticism evoked by the members of many communities, since included in the system is an instrument for eliminating the economic rent derived from development of land parcels. There is some credence to this argument but not as presented by Kmiec. We have long recognized that land rent is collectively produced, especially urban land rent through the implementation of infrastructure, and that it is privately appropriated, exchanged, and utilized. Moreover, it could be argued that it is the existence of economic rent that causes many of the conflicts over land use, and these have resulted in an ever-increasing intermediation of the state (Roweis and Scott, 1981). This issue will be discussed in greater detail later. Here the focus is on Kmiec's proposal.

The fallacy of the argument is demonstrated by neoclassical economic rent analysis. Kmiec suggests that any enhancement in land value above its use in agriculture can be taxed away without affecting land use, that is, the tax is neutral with respect to land use. He would simply require the developer to pay for the cost of infrastructure out of the unearned increment between the capitalized value of land in its agricultural use and the capitalized value of any future use discounted to the present. The value of any future use depends upon the intensity of future development, which, in turn, depends upon the selected LUI rating, the time of development, and holding costs such as interest and taxes. Any unearned increment not devoted to public improvements will be reverted to the general revenue of the community.

Land rent, however, provides the function of allocating land in an optimal way. Suppose you own a vacant lot on a street that attracts a large number of tourists each day. Your brother-in-law wants to rent the lot from you to put up a hot dog stand while someone else is willing to pay a much higher rent to you to put up a gift shop. If the entire unearned increment is to be taxed away irrespective to whom you rent the land, optimal use of the land hinges on one factor: whether or not you happen to like your brother-in-law. Moreover, the alternative use of the land really is not its use in agriculture but its next highest use, which is equivalent to a gift shop. Hence, there may be no unearned increment. Kmiec's argument is not consistent with economic analysis of land rent in a capitalistic system, although there may be ways to extract a portion of the unearned increment. A full discussion of land rent is presented in chapter 5.

INCLUSIONARY ZONING

There has been a relatively recent governmental response to the failure of the private sector to provide low- or moderate-income housing known as "inclusionary" zoning. Although it was pioneered in 1971 by Fairfax County, Virginia, the practice is most pronounced in California and, to a lesser extent, in other states [*New York Times*, August 24, 1980, Sec. 1, p. 26, col. 1]. Actually, by 1981, inclusionary programs had been adopted by 22 California localities (Ellickson 1983).

The interest in inclusionary zoning among localities in California is not difficult to understand. Local land use policies and their impact on economic development throughout the San Francisco Bay Region during the past 20 years epitomize, perhaps as well as any example, the concern over managed growth, especially suburban growth (Dowall 1982; Frech and Lafferty 1984; Johnson 1982). In California, the environmental concerns have given rise to more vigorous and complex assessments of proposals by developers. Citizens have also become better organized and more strident in their demands for environmental quality. In addition, the economic concerns manifested in Proposition 13 provided an additional argument against new community development. This combination of factors has produced strong competition among the localities in the Silicon Valley. Each locality has attempted to entice growth in the light industrial sector of a rapid growing industry as well as the accompanying commercial growth. Simultaneously, these communities attempted to maintain the quality of the living environment without increasing taxes. In the process, the localities, through land use controls, have favored single-unit family housing with moderate levels of density. The upshot, by the late 1970s, was that there was a lack of sufficient moderate- and low-income housing available within the area to accommodate the labor force necessary for the low-skilled employment of the rapid growth in a new industry. Or, conversely, the low-skilled workers could not afford the existing housing. These conflicting trends would lead to escalating housing prices. If they continued to rise, firms in many localities throughout the region would find it more difficult to remain competitive in national and international markets. To some extent, competitive factors have resulted in spin-offs from the Silicon Valley to localities in Colorado and Texas to take advantage of the availability of lower wage labor.

In recognition of this trend, several communities have adopted the practice known as "inclusionary" zoning. In essence, an inclusionary ordinance requires the developer of new housing units to set aside a certain fraction of the units for occupancy at reduced prices for moderate-income and, less often, low-income families. Proponents of these programs describe them as "inclusionary" to contrast them with the "exclusionary" policies, such as large-lot zoning, that many suburbs have adopted to hinder the development of low-cost housing.

The Structure of Inclusionary Zoning

Local governments rarely contribute their own funds to help defray the costs of including middle- and low-income families in new residential developments. With the drying up of federal funds for low-income housing, the monies for supplying low-income housing in any form are becoming nonexistent. Inclusionary zoning is, thus, a means to attempt to provide moderate- and low-income housing. In order to increase the supply of this type of housing, the private sector must be provided with some incentive. Basically, the incentive is to permit the development of a parcel of land at a higher level of density than originally permitted by the zoning ordinance for a particular land parcel. The increased profits that can be earned from higher levels of density can then be used to subsidize the moderate- or low-income housing.

It should have been apparent from the beginning that inclusionary zoning would not be a solution to the low-income housing problem. It has long been known that the least-cost single-unit family housing that can be constructed is beyond the financial reach of low-income families; low-income households simply cannot afford newly constructed housing. Nor is it realistic to believe that middle- and upper-income families will subsidize low-income housing in a competitive housing market. If middle- and upper-income housing is available at lower density levels than would exist under inclusionary zoning, which would be true in a competitive housing market, these households would not pay comparable prices for higher density houses. Inclusionary zoning is, in effect, a tax on the nonsubsidized residents of the development. It is not a tax borne by all residents of the community. However, a brief description of attempts to implement inclusionary zoning is worthwhile.

The Implementation of Inclusionary Zoning

Inclusionary requirements typically apply only to developers of residential projects, although there have been some exceptions. For example, the California Coastal Commission awarded coastal permits for the construction of hotels on two lots subject to the condition that the waterside lot be used for a "moderate-cost" motel of 200 rooms and a 50-bed youth hostel. The same waterside lot was required to be equipped with a moderate-priced coffee shop and fast food restaurant with window service, and on weekends, 15 percent of the rooms in the market-rate hotel on the nonwaterside lot had to be made available at half price to moderate-income families. Another example is when the San Francisco planning commission approved construction of a new 27-story Holiday Inn only after the developer agreed to pay more than $100,000 annually for low-income housing for a period of 20 years.[1] There are obviously many other ways inclusionary zoning could be implemented. Nevertheless, it has been primarily applied to residential housing developments.

The inclusionary requirements vary significantly among communities. For example, in California the required set-aside may range from 10 percent to 33 percent of newly constructed units, whereas in New Jersey a developer could receive density bonuses by providing 20 percent low- to moderate-income housing. Moreover, the set-aside may vary by income grouping. For example, Orange County, California, has required developers to set aside 10 percent of the units for families with income less than 80 percent of the median county income, another 10 percent for families having between 80 and 100 percent of median county income, and another 5 percent for families having between 100 and 120 percent of median county income (Ellickson 1983). Obviously, therefore, there could be as many different types of programs as there are localities with inclusionary zoning.

Although the housing subsidies made available through inclusionary programs are usually nominally directed at low- and moderate-income families, the beneficiaries primarily have been households that are normally included as middle-income. This arises from the definition of "moderate-income" used by professional housing advocates. For example, inclusionary programs define "moderate-income families" as those with incomes between 80–120 percent of the median income of families within the county. While some adjustments are made for family size, family assets, and other factors, the moderate-income group is, in effect, in the middle of the income distribution of all families. Other factors may also enter depending upon the desires of the community. Some communities extend first priority to primary wage earners employed within the community or to persons who have been residents of the community for a given period of time (Ellickson 1983).

A major equity problem occurs in the depth of the subsidies and in the selection of program beneficiaries. Inclusionary governments usually control the prices of inclusionary units to ensure that the intended beneficiaries can afford to occupy them. Since many of the families spend more of their income on housing than they would in the inclusionary units and the inclusionary units tend to be of higher quality than the housing units the beneficiaries would otherwise occupy, a chosen few become the beneficiaries of rather deep subsidies. In some cases, units have sold for two-thirds of their market value, while in other cases they have been discounted up to 50 percent.

Obviously an announcement that inclusionary units are about to become available generates large numbers of applicants, since over 50 percent of county residents usually qualify. Some inclusionary ordinances have failed to specify how the winners are to be selected but, through experience, queues and lotteries have generally come to be the most acceptable form of distribution.

Because of the extent of the subsidy involved and the small number of applicants who can benefit from the program, most officials who manage inclusionary programs also favor the imposition of resale controls. Otherwise, significant economic rent could accrue to the lucky few who are selected to occupy the units. There is, however, an adverse aspect to resale price controls.

So long as owners are aware that they will not be able to reap the economic rent at resale, and given that the market value of the unit exceeds the price of the unit to the owner, the owners have no incentive to maintain the unit. In fact, they may even have a disincentive. Depreciation will thus occur at an inordinate rate.

Prospectus

There is little doubt that, as usually practiced, inclusionary zoning is a misguided undertaking. Although originally intended to benefit low- and moderate-income families, most inclusionary units have been bestowed upon families in the middle third of the income distribution. Also, because only a small percentage of those eligible can hope to obtain the units, localities have had to resort to lotteries and queues to select the few lucky beneficiaries. This, however, should not have been a surprise. Muth reported that, in 1968, about 670,000 public housing units had been constructed nationwide. This number represented enough for only about 7 percent of all eligible families (Muth 1975: 121). When families can live in better housing at a lower price than their present residence, clearly an excess demand will occur.

Those who adhere to the inclusionary zoning argument might believe that inclusionary zoning could be used to foster integrated housing, at least integration by economic classes. However, economic models demonstrate that this is is not a valid argument. Stratification models (McGuire 1974; Henderson 1977) suggest that households will segregate (stratify) by income groups by communities. If they will attempt to stratify by community, they will obviously attempt to stratify by neighborhood. Simple casual empiricism in practically every community provides substantial credibility to neighborhood stratification. Inclusionary zoning can impact economic integration only if it is implemented so stringently that it reduces competition in the housing market to the extent that developers are no longer able to develop neighborhoods. The neighborhood and land reform movements of the 1960s and 1970s stand in sharp contrast with inclusionary zoning.

In addition, if one views inclusionary zoning as a program for income redistribution, it encounters the same economic arguments as any form of housing subsidy. In-kind housing subsidies are not an efficient method of income redistribution. As a supply-side subsidy, they do provide better housing but for only a select few.

A PROPERTY RIGHTS APPROACH

William Fischel (1985) has developed an analytical apparatus to examine land use issues that allows for a diagrammatic exposition of the establishment and exchange of entitlements. This analysis is quite consistent, in many ways, with the approach taken in chapter 3, and it provides useful insights into land use controversies. Fischel takes four chapters to develop his analysis. It is hoped that these few pages will do him justice.

The basic argument is that property rights should be viewed as an entitlement, that zoning should be alienable, and that zoning should be explicitly fungible.[2] The analysis begins with the development of an "entitlements diagram," which is a generalization of the Coase theorem, although the Coase theorem itself is not so important.

The assumptions of the Coase theorem are: (1) all entitlements are defined (measurable and exchangeable); (2) entitlements, as well as the rules by which entitlements are protected, are exclusively assigned (presumably by legislatures and courts); (3) transactions costs are nil (no legal restraints or information costs); and (4) initial distribution of entitlements does not affect subsequent demand for their exchange (Fischel 1985: 130–131).

The curves JJ' and KK' (see figure 2) are the marginal benefit schedules for restrictions both to the community and the landowner. They are also demand curves for the land to be used in particular ways. The marginal benefit schedule of the landowner for a particular parcel of land is read from right to left. At point J', there is no benefit to the landowner since he cannot sell or use the land at all. Note that KK' is a demand curve for permission of the landowner-developer to develop, for example, housing on lots of various sizes. That is, the height of KK' is determined by the demand for land for housing. Yet KK' is not the demand curve for housing. Rather, it represents the community's permission to allow development by the landlord-developer. The area under KK' denotes the dollar value to have an entitlement for the use of the land parcel from the most restrictive to the least restrictive use, for example, from lots of 10 acres in size for single-unit family housing to multiunit family housing of 10 units per acre.

The community's marginal benefit schedule JJ' is read from left to right. Its shape indicates that benefits to current residents increase with additional restrictions on undeveloped land but at a diminishing rate. The height and shape of JJ' is clearly problematic, as Fischel states. Many residents place no value on some restrictions, while others may even place negative values on certain restrictions, as, for example, those who would like to operate a business out of their home in a residential area. Moreover, many residents welcome growth and development. Most, if not all, business and professional people prefer growth, as well as many residents who hold to the notion that all growth is beneficial to the community. The shape of the marginal benefit curve to the community is, however, probably consistent over the range of restrictions in which most zoning controversies occur. Otherwise, there would be no controversy.

Given the assumptions behind figure 2, the initial assignment of entitlements on the restriction index does not matter as far as the outcome is concerned. If the initial assignment favors the landowner (point A'), the community will

Figure 2
The Entitlements Diagram to Suburban Land Use

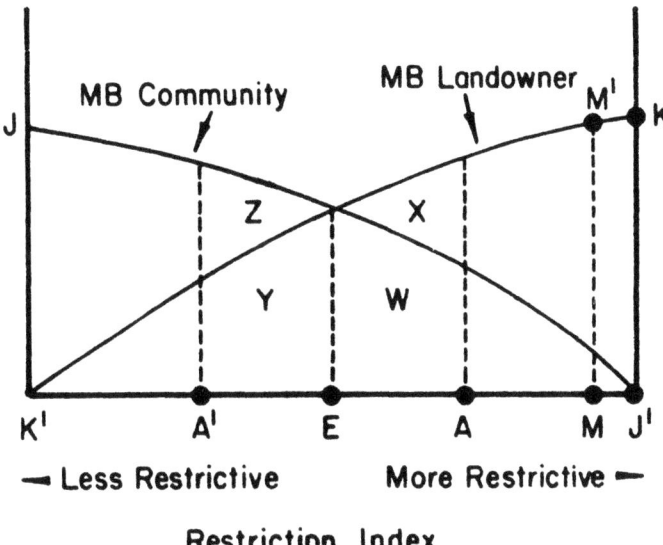

Source: Fischel, William A. 1985. *The Economics of Zoning Laws: A Property Rights Approach to American Land Use Controls.* Baltimore: Johns Hopkins Press. Reprinted with permission, p. 128.

attempt to pay the landowner to accept additional restrictions. If the landowner is protected by a liability rule, which is the normal case, the community must pay damages (Y) plus (Z), the entire consumers' surplus. If point A is initially assigned, the landowner will have to pay the community to escape the restrictions. Since the community is normally protected by a property rule, it could extract up to X + W in figure 2. In either case, after all transactions take place, point E is obtained.

Fischel argues that there is an important distinction between a liability rule and a property rule. Under a property rule, the owner of an entitlement can refuse to sell at any price. For example, the government can acquire all of the surplus by refusing permission to develop. Under a liability rule, this right is lost, and a third party monitors offers for reasonableness. The government's right of eminent domain thus falls under the definition of liability rule. Yet, as will be discussed below, Fischel simultaneously provides reasons why a property rule protection for the community will not result in the community extracting all surplus values from exchanges with landowners. It is also true that a liability rule such as eminent domain is not necessarily less costly for the government purchase of land entitlements than a property rule (Munch 1976; Polinsky 1979).

The Property Rights Approach

The assumptions behind the Coase theorem are obviously too extreme to be realistically applied. Entitlements are neither universally defined nor can they be exclusively assigned, and most transactions involving land issues are complicated and costly to arrange. Thus, the theorem itself is of little significance. Its importance is the approach that it suggests for examining land use issues. It points more clearly to the alternatives for dealing with controversial land use issues than do other economic approaches.

If the defect in zoning is seen to be an incomplete assignment of entitlements, the property rights approach leads one to ask how entitlements ought to be assigned. If the defect is high transaction costs, the approach leads one to ask how to reduce such costs. If the defect is one of fairness, it leads one to ask how entitlements should be distributed or protected so as to promote fairness (Fischel 1985: 116–117).

Fischel adopts the median voter approach in that local authorities attempt to maximize the net worth of the median voter. Actually he does not adopt a median voter approach because he strays from it on occasion.[3] Irrespective of whether it is actually a median voter approach, the analysis can proceed exactly as it does.

We now return to the entitlements diagram. Fischel believes that zoning offers initial entitlements to the community well to the right of point E. Moreover, because zoning enabling acts have generated a broad set of powers to the community and court decisions have adopted a broad view of the police power, communities are seldom required to compensate landowners whose property values are reduced by zoning. Courts do, however, protect a landowner whose land value is completely eliminated, therefore, point J' can be excluded as an entitlement.

While the Coase theorem assumes that the initial distribution of entitlements does not affect the demand for the goods being traded, this assumption does not apply in the context of land use controls. Fischel argues that it does make a difference whether point A or A' is the initial entitlement in figure 3. Even assuming zero transaction cost, the wealth effect makes a difference in the equilibrium trading point. For example, if the initial entitlements were at point A (figure 3), the resulting equilibrium would occur at point E. However, if trade began at A', the resulting equilibrium would be at point E', which is less restrictive in the density of land use. Because there could be many different initial entitlement points, obviously there could be many equilibrium points.

Fischel further argues that the wealth effect of zoning is more important in the suburbs and primarily benefits the wealthiest members of suburban society. Aside from rural landowners, the earliest residents of most developing suburbs were more affluent than the average and were among the group who first enacted zoning legislation. As a consequence, they enacted zoning ordinances that placed constraints on development that led to exclusion.

Figure 3
Wealth, Preference, and Monopoly Effects

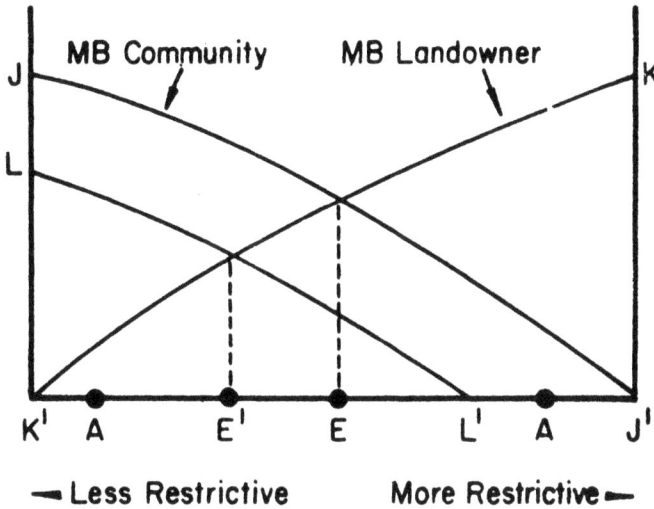

Source: Fischel, William A. 1985. *The Economics of Zoning Laws: A Property Rights Approach to American Land Use Controls.* Baltimore: Johns Hopkins Press. Reprinted with permission, p. 136.

The wealth effect can be demonstrated with two different marginal benefit schedules for the community. With a generous entitlement granted to the community, such as point A, line JJ' is the demand for restrictiveness. When the community begins at point A', where it must purchase most additional restrictions from landowners, LL' reflects the community's demand for restrictiveness. The vertical distance between JJ' and LL' thus represents a wealth effect attributable to differences in the initial assignment of entitlements. As a consequence, the wealth effect will cause a difference in the equilibrium trading point. With the community's initial entitlements at A, the resulting equilibrium will be at point E, whereas if trade is at A', the result (E') will be less restrictive.

Fischel thus believes that the wealth effect adds to the restrictions on housing and that the demand for land use controls is greatest in the wealthiest communities. Yet he admits this result would be true even if all restrictions had to be purchased, as is found in affluent suburbs with residential covenants (Fischel 1985: 137). He further suggests that the vertical distance between LL' and JJ' can be viewed as the difference between a community's valuation of "legitimate" uses for zoning and "illegitimate" uses. "Such legitimate purposes may be to prevent traditional physical nuisances, promote reasonable levels of public safety, and provide for orderly growth of the community" (Fischel 1985: 139). The nature of illegitimate preferences may vary from community to community and from one era to another. The most widely regarded illegitimate preference is a desire for racial exclusion, but, beyond this preference, there is no consensus.

Fischel concludes that welfare gains may be lost because of the monopoly aspect of local government or because transactions costs prevent further exchange. Legal impediments and public choice problems have been found to be the major sources of transactions costs. The two situations where zoning has been found to be too restrictive—the wealth effect of granting zoning entitlements to the early residents of a community and the exercise of illegitimate zoning preferences—have little to do with efficiency. In these two cases, the community and the landowner can achieve no voluntary gains through trade, although outsiders might be harmed. The general conclusion, consistent with that of most commentators, is that zoning is too restrictive.

As a means to provide a resolution, Fischel focuses on the taking issue. The just compensation aspect of the taking clause provides a remedy for the defects in zoning noted above. There are four legal approaches to the taking issue, and the problems inherent in each can be illustrated with reference to the entitlements diagram.

The clearest example of a taking involves a zoning ordinance that requires physical occupation of public access to an individual's property. The local government cannot simply zone someone's property for a recreation area or a school for the benefit of the community without compensating the landowner. This represents the physical invasion standard for determining a taking. In figure 4, such a taking is represented by a movement from A to D. But, in itself, the physical invasion standard is not sufficient.

The second legal standard for determining a taking is the diminution of value, but it is also not helpful by itself. It would prevent a movement from A to D, but it would not prevent a movement from A to C. This movement is like telling a property owner whose property is suited for commercial use that its highest density use is single-unit family housing. Clearly, zoning can and does prevent certain parcels of land from being used for the most profitable activity, but, in a literal sense, the diminution of value has not been widely applied. There are, however, a number of decisions in which the courts have emphasized the magnitude of loss to the landowner as a reason for overturning the zoning as a taking.

A third standard, only occasionally applied, is the balancing means test or the benefit cost criterion. In using this test, the judge will attempt to determine whether the public benefits created or preserved by the ordinance outweigh the costs to the landowner. Fischel believes this standard may be most appealing to economists but that it has serious drawbacks as a normative rule in taking cases. For example, using his illustration, suppose a zoning issue is not involved, but the issue concerns the acquisition of the right-of-way for the construction of a highway. The benefits of acquiring the land for the route clearly are greater than the cost of acquisition. Normally, under eminent domain, payment would be made to the landowner. Yet, by the benefit-cost standard, no payment would be

Figure 4
Zoning Entitlements and Takings

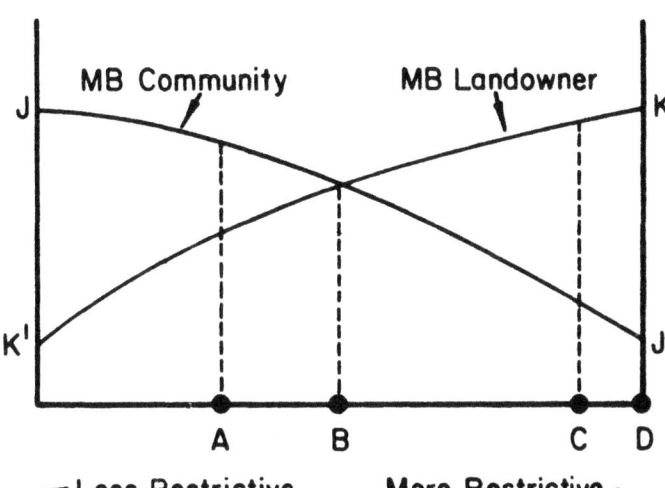

Source: Fischel, William A. 1985. *The Economics of Zoning Laws: A Property Rights Approach to American Land Use Controls.* Baltimore: Johns Hopkins Press. Reprinted with permission, p. 156.

made since the benefits exceed the costs. No payment clearly violates our normative notion of the compensation principle (Fischel 1985: 157).

The fourth standard is a harm-benefit rule. Under this standard, regulations that prevent a landowner from "harming" the public are valid, irrespective of the degree of restrictiveness. Restrictions that would create a public benefit are, however, invalid takings. Thus, individuals have no right to inflict "harms" on society, but the public in general, not just one or a few individuals, should pay for the benefits.

Fischel states that it may be surprising to the reader that he adopts a version of the harm-benefit rule called the "normal behavior" standard in determining when compensation for zoning regulations should be made. "The reasons are that it promotes economic efficiency by stabilizing expectations and reducing transaction cost of providing for public goods" (1985: 158).

Note now the similarity in Fischel's argument and that of chapter 3. Fischel argues that this notion promotes Michelman's (1967) fairness criterion. A taking will be found if the landowner could reasonably expect that he could use his land in a particular way, but the community prevented the use through its police powers. This expectation thus reduces the uncertainty of planning and investment for land use by the landowner.

What constitutes a reasonable expectation? In Fischel's words:

A reasonable expectation is . . . one that conforms to prevailing social standards of acceptable behavior.

We begin, then, with one rule for resolving the taking issue: a taking may be argued to have occurred when a regulation requires a landowner to exceed prevailing social standards of behavior. The landowner should not be forced to "confer a benefit" on the community. No taking occurs when the regulation simply forces the landowner to conform to prevailing community standards or prevents him from adopting subnormal land uses (1985: 159).

Fischel recognizes that the normal behavior standard establishes a starting point for determining a taking, but it does not provide satisfactory criteria for many zoning controversies because zoning laws change over time. Here we should distinguish between a regulation that is consistent with "normal behavior" and a regulation that moves the community towards "supernormal standards." The rule for determining taking, thus, should be that government authorities respect the entitlements of individual landowners so long as the entitlements conform to community standards. When community standards change or when normal behavior is not consistent with demands by the community, regulations that restrict the use of property beyond normal standards should compensate affected property owners unless two conditions are met: first, the cost of making the compensation is excessive relative to the amount of the compensation, and, second, public benefits from the restriction can be shown to exceed the cost to landowners.

As Fischel notes, the determination of what "normal behavior" and "community standards" are cannot be given an exact answer, although there are some guidelines. Fischel does not believe one should look at the text of the community's master plan to determine standards for normal behavior. Following Ellickson (1977: 422), a better normal behavior guideline is what the community does, not what it says. The standards that a community has imposed upon itself provide a way to examine its behavior. If a community changes its standards from normal to a standard that exceeds normal, such as a change from half-acre lots to two-acre lots for single-unit family housing, this activity should be subject to scrutiny under the taking issue. Similarly, a developer who proposes a development that exceeds what appears to be normal past development densities would not have a case for taking.

One additional suggestion offered is to look at the pattern of development in large, self-contained communities. In these communities (Planned Unit Developments, for example), the developer has an incentive to establish a mix of land uses that maximizes the benefits of initial residents and residents in a later time period—the Henderson solution of chapter 3. A note of caution should be added here. PUDs tend to have relatively low gross densities, although they may have high net densities in certain areas. PUDs, however, have not generally been developed for all income groups. Rather, their primary market has been for upper and middle income groups.

These rules are consistent with economic efficiency because they provide a set of reasonable expectations for landlord-developers. They are also consistent with Michelman's standard of fairness. Landowners should be able to perceive that the public benefits from the regulation are greater than the private costs of the regulations, and it is in the long-run interest of people like themselves.

Entitlement Exchanges

The most ambitious aspect of Fischel's work is his attempt to persuade the reader that entitlement exchanges should take place. His argument proceeds from the distinction developed by Calabresi and Melamed (1972) between property rules, liability rules, and inalienability. A property rule permits the owner of an entitlement to hold out for any price or to refuse to trade at all. A liability rule requires the owner of an entitlement to exchange the entitlement provided the offer is considered acceptable by a third party—the owner cannot refuse all offers. However, there may be occasions when entitlements should not be exchanged under any condition. This condition is referred to as inalienability.

Fischel first argues that zoning should be alienable and that it should be explicitly fungible. The basis for this argument is that, in adversarial court proceedings over land use issues, judges will not be in a position to assign entitlements at the equilibrium of the marginal benefit schedules. Judges will hear arguments from the community for point B (figure 3) and arguments for point A from the landlord-developer. How is the judge to decide? Even using normal behavior as the best guide, there is no guarantee that an optimal land use decision will be made (point E). But this does not matter. By permitting the court's right to assign entitlements consistent with normal behavior or some similar criterion, even if it is not the equilibrium, the parties will change it. Once the entitlement is established, suppose at point B, landowners would attempt to estimate, by a series of tentative offers, what the true benefit schedule of the community is so that they might buy their way out of the excessive restrictions.

Having argued for alienable zoning entitlements and alienable legal standing, Fischel considers whether entitlements should be protected by a property rule or a liability rule. The major difference is that under a property rule the owner of an entitlement can refuse to sell at any price without explanation. An example of an exercise of a property right would be a community simply refusing to rezone a parcel of land. Under a liability rule, the right of refusal is lost. The use of eminent domain in acquiring land by the public sector from the private sector perhaps best illustrates an exercise of and a need for a liability rule.

"The rule proposed here is nearly without precedent in our legal system" (Fischel 1985: 191). He proposes that supernormal community entitlements—that is, those that are more restrictive than can be justified by normal standards of land use within the community—be protected by the liability rule. There is an assumption that supernormal community rules are illegitimate public purposes and are, in effect, a desire to exclude certain persons from the community. Liability rule protection enables landlord-developers to buy their way out of inappropriate restrictions. This rule, therefore, gives the developer eminent domain to develop in the face of community opposition. A major advantage in reversing the usual entitlement protection in the supernormal range is that supernormality is the only thing in question. Courts need not be concerned with exclusionary intentions, racial motives, or monopoly power of local government in land use issues. Having established this argument, Fischel goes on to propose six rules for takings and entitlement protection (1985: 200–203).

Prospectus

Theoretically salable zoning could work in the allocation of land. Marginal benefit schedules for salable zoning rights would be no less difficult for communities to determine than they are presently determined. In setting and implementing current land use policy, communities determine the density of development. This action thus implies that communities are able to determine their marginal benefit schedule.

There are, however, obvious criticisms in permitting a community to sell zoning rights to the highest bidder, some of which Fischel notes. For example, a community that could sell rezonings might increase local revenues by establishing restrictive regulations for the purpose of selling them to the highest bidder (1985: 180).

A more fundamental criticism involves long-run optimal land use for a community. The future growth of a community will be partly guided by planned infrastructure. Certain parcels of land, therefore, should be designated for specific broad categories of use. For example, a new, major traffic artery with a major interchange will generate a demand for commercial and industrial uses in proximity to the interchange. Suppose the infrastructure changes are still in the planning stage and the landowner desires to develop the land for residential use. Under a liability rule, the community would be forced to sell zoning rights for housing. Thus, only with a property rights rule would optimal land use occur in the long run.

There is an additional problem in Fischel's model. Recall from chapter 2 that there are at least five "common" types of conflicts between the community and landlord-developers that can create controversial zoning issues, not all of which are resolved through a pure median voter approach. Those conflicts that are site-specific would require only adjacent property owners or neighborhoods to reveal their marginal benefit schedules. While unanimous approval by individual households within a neighborhood for salable property rights would probably be impossible, a resolution to site-specific conflicts might be accomplished through a neighborhood property rights approach such as proposed by Nelson. However, if salable zoning such as proposed in Nelson's neighborhood property rights approach is permitted, the land use desires of the neighborhood may not be consistent with those of the median voter. Therefore, even if a system of salable zoning were put into effect, conflicts will arise that require some form of third party intervention or mediation.

It is interesting to note the consistency between the policy implications of Fischel's model and the model presented in chapter 3. Fischel is concerned about land use restrictions that exceed what could be considered normal land use densities. It is only when the distribution of initial entitlements permits a wealth effect to occur that salable zoning would lead to a higher density of land use. Yet he argues that the distribution of initial entitlements should be determined by historical growth patterns. The element of surprise is thus eliminated, and fairness to both residents and landlord-developers results. In effect, therefore, the wealth effect does not occur so long as development densities do not exceed past densities. Consequently, land use controversies would not arise.

A major problem, which will be more fully developed in chapter 5, is that at some stage in suburban growth developers desire development with densities that exceed past growth, while residents desire to maintain a suburban ambience. A change in initial entitlements at this stage results in a wealth effect for landlord-developers, not residents. Fischel argues for normal growth by historical community standards. Interestingly, that is exactly what Petaluma and Ramapo were attempting to do, yet many believe these communities were being exclusionary.

NOTES

1. *Los Angeles Times,* January 31, 1981, Sec. 1, p. a, cols. 1, 2.

2. Perhaps the earliest version of salable zoning was provided by Marion Clawson (1960).

3. See also reviews by Fred S. McChesney in *Southern Economic Journal,* April 1986, and Gary D. Libecap in *Journal of Economic Literature,* June 1986.

5
Major Land Use Issues and Finalizing a Model for Land Use

A major purpose of this work is to provide an economic and legal rationale for land use regulation in a market economy. The rationale derives from a theoretical economic model in which a contract must be formed between residents in one time period and landlord-developers in another time period in order to achieve optimal land use. The contractual arrangement can be formed but only through a third party—the local government. In administrative law, there is legal justification for this type of contractual arrangement. The arrangement does require public intervention, that is, regulation in the market for land is necessary to form the contract.

For the most part, the analysis has focused on suburban growth, especially those communities that have experienced relatively rapid rates of development. Throughout this work, it has been argued that efficiency and equity can best be closely approximates an optimal land use model. This is clearly not the case. There are questions yet to be resolved, and there are improvements in the existing institutional structure that can enhance land use policy and land use implementation. For example, we have yet to discuss the issue that land use regulation may be a means of social control that has recently emerged in the literature. In addition, we have not addressed the problems of providing open space within a community, the preservation of environmentally sensitive land, the fact that zoning does not work well in areas in transition, and the most thorny of all, the exclusionary argument. These issues are followed by a discussion of resource allocation and land use and a conclusion.

Before proceeding to the major land use issues, no discussion of land use would be complete without an analysis of land rent. Actually, land rent may be the ultimate root of the conflict between landlord-developers and the local governing body backed by local citizens. It is, however, an elusive concept.

LAND RENT

Land rent and the broader concept of economic rent are among the most nebulous concepts with which economists attempt to deal. Yet they have long drawn the attention of economists and would-be land reformers. Beginning with the pathbreaking work in spatial economics of von Thünen (1826–33) and advanced by Weber (1928), Lösch (1954), Hoover (1937), Dunn (1954), and Isard (1956), location theory suggests that the uses of specific parcels of land are determined by economic rent. In these models, the allocation of land is determined by the amount of economic rent accruing to land because of location factors. Optimum resource allocation—in this context, optimal land use—occurs when land is put to its "highest and best use," that is, when land receives the greatest amount of economic rent. In the neoclassical models of the city and land rent as presented by Alonso (1964), Mills (1972), and Muth (1969), rent is exclusively a differential attributable to production costs (primarily transportation) at different locations, assuming freely competitive prices in all markets including both product and input markets. This produces the familiar concept of differential rent where marginal producers pay no rent since, at the margin, price equals the marginal cost of production.

Given a perfectly inelastic supply of land, clearly the distinguishing feature of land rent is that it is a surplus that is different from other factor prices in that it does not influence the supply of land. In the classical sense, land rent could therefore be taxed away without affecting aggregate supply. Consequently, the tax is neutral with respect to resource allocation. But factor prices serve two functions. Besides calling forth the aggregate supply, they ration it among competing ends. Rent serves the second function in the same manner as other factor prices. That is, it cannot be taxed away without affecting the use of land.

For example, from the neoclassical perspective, rent arises because the fixed supply of land is scarce relative to demand, it performs an allocative role, and it cannot be taxed away by a lump-sum tax without distorting land use. There is the typical argument that the alternative use for a prime urban site is its value in agricultural use and the difference between the agricultural value and the going market value can be taxed away. However, this argument is not defensible. The alleged rental component of the return to a particular site simply cannot be identified—the alternatives are arbitrary. There is a range of alternative uses of a particular parcel of land, and the decomposition of the returns called land rent and what are typically labeled transfer earnings depends entirely upon the specified alternative use. As the specified alternative use approaches the present use, land rent dissipates. That is, returns to a productive factor that are economic rent in the short run convert into payments necessary to bring forth additional services of the factor in the long run, and all payments become a cost to the purchaser of land and income to the seller. In neoclassical analysis, rent is thus a payment necessary to ensure optimal resource allocation.[1]

It is obvious that land rent adds to the cost of housing and that there are distributional aspects of rent that economists have not given high priority. As Allan Schmid (1968: 34) states, "Here the ghost of Henry George becomes more active and ideas of capturing for the public the 'unearned' increment take on new life." Good empirical estimates of the dollar value of land rent are not available, but it is apparent that it ranges from relatively minor in many communities, especially rural areas, to a figure that approaches $1 million an acre in large metropolitan areas. One study suggests that, in 1960, the net appreciation of raw land prices above the agricultural value for a sample of 130 cities with a mean population of 308,872 was 1,238 percent and 1,466 percent for 260 cities with a mean population of 180,498 (Schmid 1968: 51). However, these are gross values, that is, they contain significant development costs, primarily infrastructure such as sewer, water, and roads in addition to rent.

It is apparent, however, that landlord-developers are able to capture significant land rent above the conversion costs from agricultural to urban land. Hypothetically, a landlord-developer may have $20,000 invested in a parcel of land for a single-unit family house that contains the returns to all investment including holding cost and a normal profit; yet, given the derived demand the parcel may sell for $40,000. The $20,000 difference simply reflects the ability of the landlord to capture the present value of expected future land prices that reflect future rents. They are captured by the landlord and become a cost to the purchaser of the lot. If they were not captured by the landlord, they would be captured by the original purchaser of the lot.

Where the ghost of Henry George comes back is that some of the factors that give rise to the hypothetical $20,000 rental value have been created, in a sense, by the community. They may be in the form of infrastructure that permits the conversion of rural land to urban land, or they may be in the form of amenities of one community or even a neighborhood that are above the norm of surrounding areas. In any event, they are viewed by local citizens as being created by society in general and, therefore, could be taxed away without distorting the allocation of land.

As Fischel suggests, however, we might quibble about the meaning of "create." While landowners do not create the rental values of their land, neither does the government if the verb create denotes purposeful and directed activity (Fischel 1985: 200). Even if governments do create land values, and if it is useful to make rewards in proportion to the enhancement in land value that is attributable to the creativity, it does not make the outcome fair. "Even economists who are solicitous of private property rights concede that there is no moral connection between productivity and deservingness" (Fischel 1985: 200).

The crux of the argument goes back to the original rationale found in the taking issue. Opponents of managed growth or any form of land use regulation argue that local governments use regulation as a means whereby a majority of voters extract benefits from owners of undeveloped land. It is not a tax, but it amounts to the same thing. Moreover, they further argue that this is not consistent with the philosophy behind a democratic government.

As will become apparent in the remaining parts of this chapter, local land use regulation may not be a form of extracting a benefit from landowners of undeveloped land for the benefit of existing residents. Rather, it may be a form of maintaining the initial investment in which there was an element of rent to the landlord that became a cost to residents. The ghost of Henderson's analysis returns.

The policy implications of this analysis illustrate the nebulous properties of land rent. Even if the supply of urban land were perfectly inelastic, land rent represents a payment to a factor that helps produce optimal land use although it is unearned. Perhaps just as important is that the supply of urban land is not perfectly inelastic in the long run. Although a full discussion of the supply of urban land is left for the final chapter, it is clear that the short-run inelasticity of specific parcels of urban land gives rise to "rent seeking" (Krueger 1974; Buchanan, Tollison, and Tullock 1980). That is, it provides the impetus for members of society to attempt to gain the unearned increment. An additional policy implication will be brought out in the section on resource allocation in this chapter. However, before proceeding to a discussion of optimal resource allocation and land use, it will be helpful to discuss the major land use issues.

LAND USE REGULATION AS SOCIAL CONTROL

Recent contributions to the literature suggest the increasing significance of socioeconomic factors among community residents in land use issues. It might well be that residents have used the protection of the health, safety, and well-being of the community to include such things as the protection of the environment, but even further to include some protection from spillover effects of land use in what might fall into the vague category of aesthetics of the community.

It is clearly true of the neighborhood, but its range may easily extend to the entire community. These feelings of residents may be deep rooted since the ambience of the community may affect the self-definition of the residents and their sense of control over their lives. If this is a valid interpretation and if land use spillovers are primarily a matter of aesthetics, we can expect constant pressure for regulation at the local level (C. Rose 1984).

Carol Rose has suggested another reason why land use controls are almost always placed at the local level.

The symbolic meaning and values attached to aesthetic tastes vary enormously and are based on polycentric criteria not easily standardized. It may be that we do not want to entrust decisions about such matters to coalition-building legislatures at all, preferring those decisions to be made by people we trust because we have chosen to live with them, and because we sense our influence on them (Rose 1984: 315).

It also appears that we prefer to make these decisions on an individual basis, that is, we prefer piecemeal land use decision making. Because growth is an evolutionary process—that is, some types of changes may not be predictable— we prefer piecemeal decision making.[2] Communities are also increasingly requesting to have some knowledge of the specifics of a particular development prior to granting a zoning change. Rose makes the analogy to education, which we have regularly entrusted to localities. Here we have preferred to leave the education of our children to those whose judgment we can trust and influence rather than have the decision made through coalition-building. These are examples in which quality becomes a major criterion and does lend credence to the aesthetic aspect of land use policy and decision making being left to local jurisdictions.

These notions are also consistent with the reasons that Nelson (1984) views the neighborhood movement of the 1970s as being remarkable in many ways. It is the neighborhood that now seems attractive because it offers virtues that are threatened by modern society: cohesiveness of moral values, close personal ties, mutual trust, permanence, and stability. There is no longer the confidence that the nation is capable of fulfilling this role. With a declining sense of national community, interest is instead reviving in local and private forms of community association.

Fischel (1985) takes the notion a step further. While neighborhood segregation by income groups is common throughout the world, deliberate attempts to exclude low-income people from an entire community have arisen in the latter half of this century in the United States. Yet suburban antipathy to low-income housing has little to do with the physical structures of the housing, with perhaps the exception of mobile homes. Fischel cites the fact that low-income housing for the elderly is seldom resisted. Rather, it is a fear of crime and the threatening conduct by occupants of the housing that motivates their resistance. The principal reason for this aversion is that as a society we have lost some of our ability to control public behavior. As a consequence, society seeks alternative means to live in a community that does not have such negative spillovers. We could hire more and better trained police but that is costly. Many communities have discovered that land use controls are a less expensive means of achieving social controls.

There is a common theme that runs through each of these arguments, and it has been expressed in other ways by commentators for several years.[3] Toll even suggests that the New York City ordinance adopted in 1916 had the objective of ensuring that today's neighborhood will be a neighborhood tomorrow (1969: 186). Some portions of the foregoing arguments are also more applicable to communities that are in close proximity to major metropolitan areas than to those that are part of medium-sized metropolitan areas. This notion will be dealt with in the following section.

There is, moreover, an additional aspect to the increasing concern by members of many communities over land use issues, especially those who reside in communities in the path of urban growth of metropolitan areas of almost any size. These include many of the California communities that have given rise to numerous exclusionary studies, as well as the majority of sunbelt areas. The notion basically goes back to Henderson's contribution that optimality in land use requires a contract between the residents in time period one and the landlord-developer (which must become the local government because of the public-good argument) in time period two.

Optimal land use thus requires that both residents and landlord-developers are able to achieve their highest utility level. The term "optimal land use" also implies that land use is efficient. However, as discussed in chapter 3, one must be aware that efficiency in land use means different things to different people. To some developers, optimal suburban land use means developing the land at urban density levels, without regard for traffic congestion and visual amenities. Yet, there is a distinction between a suburban environment and an urban environment. Suburban communities have an ambience distinct from the urban environment. If residents are to achieve their highest level of utility, they must have some assurance of the ambience in time period two in order to determine the price in time period one. The character of the community may change, but it is their desire that it remain suburban. Suburban neighborhoods provide residents with the cohesiveness of moral values, permanence, and stability.

THE MERITS OF LAND USE REGULATION

Economic models suggest that, given the heterogeneity of preferences and income of groups of people, stratification among communities in which different levels of services are provided will occur. Moreover, the optimal solution for both households and the landlord-developer requires a contract between time period one and time period two, but, for this to be obtained, regulation is required because of the inability of these two groups to reach a solution through the private market.

From a planning perspective, several factors suggest the need for regulation. First, optimal resource allocation requires optimal utilization of urban infrastructure. It is through the planning process that the location of the infrastructure is determined, especially the transportation system and sewer and water services. Although for many counties the state or municipality provides the major road network within a community, the specific location of future roads is determined cooperatively by the locality and the agency for road construction. Moreover, while sewer systems are often heavily subsidized by federal monies, their location is determined at the local level. Optimal utilization of future infrastructure obviously depends upon the future use of land. This is especially true with respect to the major categories of land use, that is, commercial, industrial, and residential. The segregation of land uses for future development can be achieved only through some form of regulation.

Second, from a planning perspective, the pervasiveness of negative spillovers without regulation is all too real. Those who believe the negative spillover argument is overrated need only talk to anyone who has been involved in the implementation of land use policies. Even with zoning ordinances, what individual property owners and some landlord-developers request in the way of zoning changes, variances, or special-use permits for particular parcels of land continues to stretch the imagination. There are many variations to the old story of a request for a funeral home in a single-unit family neighborhood: an automobile junk yard adjacent to a single-unit family neighborhood in an area designated for low-density housing; a mobile home park to be located on a prime commercial site between a multimillion dollar motel complex and a similar project in the planning stage; and requests to construct high-density multiunit housing projects that abut single-unit housing neighborhoods for the sole purpose of rent seeking, that is, to take advantage of the amenities of the adjacent neighborhoods. Note that these are site-specific illustrations. One could also make a strong argument that the social reasons behind land use controls are a significant part of the negative spillover effect, if we include the deterioration of the ambience of the community as a negative spillover.

The question that cannot be resolved, at least at this time, is the extent to which communities have the right to manage growth. Henderson's analysis demonstrates that for residents to achieve their highest level of utility, the contract between time period one and time period two implies growth management. That is, landlord-developers in period one are not in a position to form the contract between the two time periods. As a consequence, they are in a position to reap an economic return expected in time period two that exceeds the return in time period one if the community has amenities above the average for communities within the area. This is precisely why the residents in time period one need a contract; otherwise, they are exploited in time period two. The landlord-developers and, through voice in the political process, the residents created the ambience of the community in time period one that carried over into time period two. It is just as true that landlord-developers need a contract between time period one and time period two in order to prevent residents of the community from making land use changes that were not predicted. This creates the need for third-party intervention—the public sector—which leads to managed growth.

This is not to imply that managed growth need be exclusionary with respect to income groups; it probably does imply that managed growth will be somewhat exclusionary with respect to overall levels of density and with respect to certain types of commercial or industrial growth. If we can agree that societal values with respect to the community are important, just as the Supreme Court has agreed that we have a right to live in single-unit family neighborhoods, then this should be taken into consideration in adopting land use policy.

The land use model presented in chapter 3 attempts to accomplish the incorporation of the right to manage growth in a manner that does not lead to exclusion by income groups. The comprehensive plan segregates land uses by major category: commercial, industrial, and residential. This segregation is accomplished taking into consideration the existing structure of the community, existing infrastructure, and planned infrastructure. Using natural and man-made boundaries, the reduction in negative spillover effects from major use categories can be and has been successfully accomplished in many communities.

There is a major distinction between residential land use in the comprehensive plan in this model and residential land use as it currently exists in the comprehensive plans of most communities. Zoning preceded planning. As a result, all land in those communities that have adopted zoning is zoned for some purpose. For example, such undeveloped land either idle or in agricultural or forestry use can be developed for residential use, albeit probably at a low level of density. That is, although the land may be zoned for agricultural use, all development is not prohibited. Some of this land may lie within the land designated for residential use within the comprehensive plan. In the comprehensive plan in this model, the undeveloped land designated for residential use should not be zoned in any particular manner. The specific zone attached to each parcel will occur when the landlord-developer decides to develop. This serves two purposes. First, it prohibits communities from prezoning residential land. In effect, therefore, communities could not prezone all, or even large segments, of undeveloped land for large-lot, single-unit family housing. The same argument should also apply to industrial land since some communities often prezone more land for industrial use than normal industrial use suggests. Second, it retains the flexibility necessary for piecemeal land use implementation. The specific zone for each parcel is thus determined on the merits of each zoning request. In addition, the existence of the comprehensive plan provides the first part of the contract between the residents in time period one and time period two as well as for the landlord-developer. Communities may desire, however, to designate at least portions of the land for residential use into categories such as low- and moderate-density levels in order to strengthen the contract.

The basic premise behind the criticism of zoning is that it produces a redistribution of wealth in favor of upper income groups at the expense of lower income groups. This presupposes that upper income groups gain control of the political process, which they use to exercise exclusionary practices. While exclusion may occur in some communities, most communities do not attempt to exclude low-income households and many attempt to provide low-income housing. Exclusion does occur when the location of subsidized low-income housing creates negative spillovers in adjacent neighborhoods. However, the absence of exclusion does imply that sufficient undeveloped land area is available within the community for natural or man-made buffers to exist to eliminate the spillover. In many growing communities, such land is available. Many suburban communities do exclude, if by exclusion we focus on density. A reading of the land reform movement suggests that suburbanites are attempting to maintain the ambience of the community, yet clearly recognizing that growth will change the character of the community. Cluster housing, zero lot line construction, apartments, condominiums, or town houses are not excluded. Gross density, not net density, is the major concern in residential development to many suburbanites. When a developer requests high net levels of density—for example, a cluster housing development—larger setbacks and a certain amount of open space may be required for the development. This may even vary from parcel to parcel and may depend upon several factors including the natural amenities of the terrain within the parcel as well as the availability of infrastructure.

From an economic and a planning perspective, there is thus a sound basis for land use regulation that includes managed growth. In addition, there is a tradition in American political thinking that legitimizes local decision making by reference to the smallness of local communities as opposed to the largeness of the extended public. The proper mode for ensuring reasonableness, in the sense of fairness and due consideration, is in the refinement of the local potential for voice and exit. As previously discussed, local government should not be made to act like a court when it cannot act like a legislature. As the elements of this reasonableness standard, the test of due consideration should be based on participation by members of the community in the process, and the test of fairness can be based on predictability. The test of predictability is made effective in two ways. Rose suggests that it is made effective by the opportunity for exit. In this model, it is also made effective through the comprehensive plan. Although the plan should be continually updated, it provides both residents and landlord-developers with reasonable expectations of future growth. Moreover, continual update of the plan would tend to prevent unexpected changes in land uses, that is, those types of changes in policy for which compensation should be paid.

METHODS TO ENHANCE LAND USE REGULATION

Open Space and Environmentally Sensitive Land Areas

As stated at the beginning of this chapter, land use regulation, as it is practiced today, will not provide optimal land allocation. It is especially true if zoning or the comprehensive plan is used to control open space or to protect nonessential, but desired, environmentally sensitive areas. The problem is how to protect critical natural areas and preserve open space to provide a high-quality environment, yet at the same time accommodate legitimate demands for growth and development. Generally, the argument has been based on an aesthetic notion to preserve scenic areas. Although preserving scenic areas may be important, it is not so critical as to justify restrictive regulation. However, it may be that wise use of open space is beneficial to enhancing community ambience. Open-space breaks in an otherwise endless stretch of subdivisions are important to the psychological well-being of members of many communities.

There are two major categories of open spaces. One is the open areas within a neighborhood that relate to housing density. The most common connotation of open space, however, refers to undeveloped land such as agricultural land, forests, or woods. In fact, forests and woods are often referred to as passive recreation areas.

Open spaces within neighborhoods do not present a problem. Gross density levels of housing on particular parcels of land are known to members of the community and landlord-developers. If a developer desires to construct condominiums or town houses in an area of the community designated for low-density housing, the net density of a part of the parcel may be very high, but the gross density of the entire parcel can conform to low-density housing, leaving a part of the parcel in open space, perhaps even a passive recreation area. It may be that the developer is permitted to build at a level of density somewhat higher than designated by the comprehensive plan if larger-than-normal buffers are provided. This is a simple means of internalizing the spillover.

The provision of passive open space or simply the desire by members of a community to prevent development is a different issue. A community should not be permitted to designate land as open space—this represents taking without due compensation. There are, however, two ways in which a community can have access to open space. One, the community can purchase the land. Most often this quickly reveals the community's marginal benefit schedule to be substantially lower than that of the landowner. A second alternative, yet one that few communities have considered, is to purchase the rights to develop from the landowner. Public purchases of development rights to provide open space have been used in a few places, Long Island being the most notable example. This method of providing open space forces the members of a community to reveal their marginal benefit schedule, that is, they are put in the position of determining how much they would be willing to pay to protect open spaces. Public purchase of development rights, especially to provide passive recreation areas or to protect aesthetic qualities, thus provides an equitable solution.

Many critical environmental areas are at present protected by federal, regional, and state agencies. Yet there are sensitive, unprotected areas in many communities, although there is often disagreement over the degree to which the environment may be endangered by development. In many cases, quasi and formal arrangements involving the transfer of development rights can provide a solution to the preservation of sensitive, unprotected areas. A quasi arrangement can be reached through simple barter between the developer and the local government. The barter solution is often used by permitting higher-than-normal density uses in one area of a parcel of land if the developer provides protection to the environmentally sensitive area of the parcel.

A more formal transfer of development rights solution would involve actual sale or transfer of development rights as described in chapter 4. For example, when the issue is purely local in nature, such as the protection of an historical monument to which only members of the locality are particularly sensitive, a transfer of development rights provides an excellent solution.

Areas in Transition

Areas in transition are areas that at one time reflected efficient land allocation, but, as growth and development occurred, the existing use of certain land parcels no longer meets the efficiency criteria. Perhaps the classic examples are the older, single-unit family neighborhoods that should now be devoted to a higher level of density such as commercial uses or multi-unit family housing. The problem arises in that the implicit assumption of most neighborhoods, as reflected in the design of zoning, is that they will always remain the same. Local residents tend to be very conservative about their own neighborhoods. Land use, however, is constantly evolving; consequently, some neighborhoods will always be in a transition stage from one type of use to another. Thus zoning, even when complemented with the comprehensive plan, does not work well in areas in transition.

A problem exists in that zoning, as now implemented, tends to favor the existing land use; hence it may significantly slow the evolutionary change. In this sense, zoning has been criticized as being inflexible. There is also an additional problem. When the pressures for a zoning change eventually bring about the change, all landowners within the neighborhood are not equally affected. Some may be located so as to derive significant economic benefit, while others may be exposed to a negative spillover. Nothing says the change will be equitable. Moreover, there are always those within any residential area who do not want the area to change irrespective of the obvious advantages from the overall viewpoint of efficient land use.

In these situations, Nelson's analysis of neighborhood property rights provides an excellent solution. It obviously provides for a more equitable solution when some members of a neighborhood receive large gains while others are negatively affected. However, it will not satisfy those residents of the neighborhood whose psychic value of their home exceeds a normal market value. As is true with land regulation, Nelson's neighborhood property rights approach is Kaldor-Hicks efficient when psychic income is included. While it is argued in chapter 3 that a total land reform movement to private neighborhoods is not a viable solution to land use, it does represent an excellent solution to neighborhoods in transition and could be implemented within the present institutional structure of land use.

THE EXCLUSIONARY ARGUMENT

There is no doubt that the primary criticism of land use regulation, as it is exercised today, results from the implementation of zoning ordinances in such a way that they exclude certain members from a community. As a consequence, the critics contend that zoning has been used to redistribute wealth in favor of upper income groups at the expense of lower income groups. Moreover, there is empirical verification that land use restrictions have helped to raise the cost of housing, although the majority of the evidence has resulted from studies of California communities, especially in the San Francisco Bay Area.[4]

The important issue, however, is the impact of land use restrictions on land values. As pointed out by Fischel (1985), there is a conceptual problem in focusing on housing prices. The key to evaluating both the effects and desirability of zoning is the impact on undeveloped land values. That is, does zoning create higher land values that are capitalized into higher housing prices that exceed the benefits from zoning? Yet such studies have been few primarily because it is difficult to get a good sample of land sales that separate other effects. Peterson (1974 a and b) did attempt to estimate the losses to landowners who were restrained from building at higher levels of density or prevented from converting single-unit family housing to two-family structures and the corresponding gains to the community (fiscal protection and amenity values) from the restraints. His analysis suggests that landowner losses exceeded the sum of the community gains. Frech and Lafferty's (1984) study for California also finds similar results. Yet it has also been shown that communities can efficiently maximize total land value (Brueckner 1979, 1982; Lind 1973; Sonstelie and Portney 1978).

These studies and the results are important but not so much for the discussion here. No one can deny that land use regulation, as implemented in many suburban communities, leads to a lower population density than would occur in a free market. What is difficult to understand is what type of land use the critics of zoning would prefer. Only those with an extreme view favor discriminatory exclusion, and, even so, this is a moot issue since this form of exclusion is prevented by the Constitution. It is also evident that some form of exclusion will occur in any of the alternative proposals for implementing land use changes that include the market mechanism: a more structured system of covenants combined with the free market contains exclusionary characteristics, and a system using development right transfers or something comparable could become even more exclusionary than the existing system. There are also several disadvantages to each of the alternatives discussed in chapter 4. Moreover, none of the alternatives nor the existing system can solve a major criticism directed at land use, namely, the provision of low-income housing. As previously noted, we have long known that the least-cost newly constructed housing that can be provided by the private sector is out of the reach of low-income families. Yet commentators continue to employ this issue as a criticism of zoning. Surely it is time we view this criticism as a canard.

Perhaps it would be useful to construct the type of community that would exist if there were no land use regulations. It would probably be an extension of what all neighborhoods would be like if there were only one community. In a perfectly free market—that is, one in which there are absolutely no land use regulations, private or public—the residential use of land can be easily constructed. Assume that neighborhoods develop through time, that is, they are not completely developed over a short period of time. If so, all neighborhoods will eventually become similar with respect to housing type and to the distribution of income of residents within the neighborhood. As neighborhoods develop through time, any neighborhood that has amenities above the average of all neighborhoods will move toward the average. If a neighborhood begins with the development of single-unit family housing, it will be profitable for a developer to construct multiunit family housing within the neighborhood to take advantage of any amenities above the average of all neighborhoods. The rich may always try to exit and form a new neighborhood, but they soon will be followed by all other income groups. Probably the only way to prevent this from occurring is for some type of communal ownership to develop with a leasing arrangement for individual plots.

By the same logic, except realistically assuming that neighborhood stratification will occur (for example, through a system of private covenants), suburban communities within a metropolitan area would become homogeneous. That is, so long as any one community had amenities above the norm, with free entry new development would occur in a manner that would move the community toward the norm. Each community would, therefore, contain a variety of neighborhoods of all income groups that could afford new or relatively new housing. Yet, even this would not eliminate the exclusionary argument.

First, it would not satisfy those who adhere to the opening up of the suburbs movement. For example, Anthony Downs (1973) believes that the only cure to a major social problem in the United States is a completely integrated society. In terms of equity with respect to a living environment, one cannot disagree. However, it is not a realistic alternative. In order to accomplish such a movement would require substantial public outlays as well as regulatory reform since two major problems must be overcome. One, the poor would not move without subsidies, and the subsidies must be large enough for the housing and the provision of services of the host community to be acceptable. Second, each suburban community would have to agree to accept a fair share of low-income housing.

There is, however, a more realistic aspect to the exclusionary argument that has its roots in the fundamental issue of property rights. The criticisms of land regulation are directed at the suburbs of major metropolitan areas. It is apparent that the critics of suburban land management believe exclusion occurs when suburban communities do not permit residential development to approach the density levels of urban areas. Irrespective of the negative spillover argument, if residential and commercial density levels everywhere approached urban density levels, exclusion would not be a concern. This leads to the fundamental issue of property rights, private and public.

Managed Growth: Theories of Property, Private and Public

The fundamental question involved in the issue of managed growth is the issue of defining property rights. Under our system of government, the U.S. Supreme Court must decide to what extent the U.S. Constitution permits federal, state, or local governments to limit the use of private property through regulation. The crux of the issue is whether contemporary interpretations of private property rights produce a "better" society than earlier interpretations.

It is obvious that the framers of our Constitution had a strong dedication to the right of private property; it was often referred to as a natural and inalienable right. American and English intellectual leaders in the seventeenth and eighteenth centuries deemed the right of private property as a bulwark against authoritarianism. It provided freedom, autonomy, and independence to the average citizen and they argued that, if the government could take away something owned by the individual, it could exert enormous power over people.

One would be reluctant to speak, write, pray, or petition in a manner displeasing to the authorities, lest one lose what has already been legally acquired. Consequently, property was a foremost personal right because the exercise of many other rights depended upon it.... If government wanted to acquire their property, at least it would have to pay for it (Siegan 1982: 360).

Siegan points out that three of the most able jurists this country has produced were no less positive about property rights. He offers some of their comments in this regard:

John Marshall: The nature of society and government limits the legislative power. But where are they to be found if the property of the individual, fairly and honestly acquired, may be seized without compensation?
Joseph Story: That government can scarcely be deemed to be free, where the rights of property are left solely dependent upon the will of a legislative body, without any restraint. The fundamental maxims of a free government seem to require, that the rights of personal liberty and private property be held sacred.
James Kent: The natural and active sense of property ... leads to the cultivation of the earth, the institution of government, the acquisition of the comforts of life, the growth of the useful arts, the spirit of commerce, the productions of taste, the erections of charity, and the display of the benevolent affections (1982: 363).

Siegan's conclusion is simply that the Supreme Court, in confirming the powers of local zoning, has repudiated a principle that was foremost in the minds of many of the framers of the Constitution. This is apparently true. Yet even Blackstone was aware that property could not be used and enjoined without control or diminution in value for the good of the whole community save only by the laws of the land. As long as there is an abundant supply of land and the use of land by one does not harm that of another, most would agree with the words of the great jurists. But this is a different era and notions with respect to private property can and should change. It is through the Supreme Court that a changing attitude toward property rights is reflected. This notion will be further developed in the following section.

Roger Pilon argues that, in the intervening years, the attitude of society toward land use has come to succeed court, precedent, and reason, and the earlier insights have gradually been lost. A new theory has emerged that pits property rights against so-called people rights.

Accordingly, it views private property not as a condition of freedom but as an outright impediment to freedom . . . a theory that argues that private property is something not to be secured but to be abolished—or better to be collectivized. [Thus what we have are two theories]—the theory of private property and individual freedom, and the theory of public property and collective freedom (Pilon 1982: 373).

In applying the notion of collective property rights to the taking issue, the question is when is the state required to compensate those it regulates. As Pilon argues, first, if the activity violates a right, such as the criminal use of a gun, it is illegitimate to begin with, and no compensation is required. Second, if the activity is legitimate, the state has no right to prohibit it, but when the state does prohibit an activity in order to achieve some "public good," compensation is required.

Probably most would agree, but we are right back where we started. The crux of the argument is what is an illegitimate taking. For example, Pilon states that "similarly, except when issues of endangerment arise, regulations of lot sizes, setback requirements, or restrictions on types of construction are all illegitimate. For the prohibited uses, were they permitted would take nothing that belongs to others and hence would violate no rights" (1982: 386).

This is simply not true. Why should we not have rights to prevent certain spillovers? The city of Williamsburg, Virginia, in which Colonial Williamsburg, a major tourist attraction, is located, has a height restriction on buildings. Suppose a 20–story motel were constructed adjacent to this historical area, which has been reproduced for the benefit of the public not only to view but to acquire some sense or feel for the founding of our nation, where the founding fathers worked, and what their life-style in the colonial capital was like. Obviously, the ambience of the restored area would be significantly reduced if a modern high-rise building were visible. Yet without the restriction, it would occur. This does not constitute a taking. Colonial Williamsburg Foundation created the ambience, which further created a positive spillover for a large tourist-related industry and it is being protected by a regulation.

A landlord-developer owns a large parcel of undeveloped land that is in the path of growth in a suburban community. A major four-lane highway is planned to cross the parcel, and a major interchange is to be constructed within the parcel. Before the community will grant a rezoning of the parcel from agricultural to mixed commercial, industrial, and residential uses, the landlord-developer is expected to donate the land for the right-of-way and the interchange. This is not an illegitimate requirement and does not constitute a taking. The value of the parcel will be enhanced threefold, at least, as a result of public expenditure that will be privately appropriated.

A community has designated a large section of undeveloped or partly developed land area for residential housing. Because the main transportation artery was initially constructed for rural use and will not be adequate when completely developed, although it may be 20 years hence, developers are expected to donate sufficient right-of-way and provide adequate setbacks for future road expansion. This is not an illegitimate regulation, although it might fall under the category of endangerment.

These are just a few of many different types of illustrations that demonstrate that the pure private-property-right approach to land use will not produce optimal land allocation and will obviously produce spillovers even when combined with covenants, the often-suggested alternative. The Supreme Court has recognized that a collective property right approach—that is, regulation combined with the free market—is a legitimate exercise of the police power provided in the Constitution. Here there is a gray area. Sometimes the use of the collective property right approach through regulation creates a taking, but it is through the court system that the rules should be established.

OPTIMAL RESOURCE ALLOCATION AND LAND USE

Boundary Effects

The basic conflict is clearly framed. As urban areas increase in population, they tend to expand with two different boundary effects. One is an expansion of the suburban boundary into the rural areas. This is often met with mixed emotions by the rural or semirural community. For example, in some of the communities of the Washington, D.C., western suburbs, relatively wealthy, large landowners may desire to maintain the rural ambience, even to the extent of retaining dirt roads. As the pressure for growth increases, these communities may attempt to provide relatively low levels of density. In other agricultural areas, farmers may welcome growth as land prices are bid up and they have no interest in the density of development. It is in these areas that suburbanites gain political control and attempt to maintain the suburban ambience as growth pressures mount.

The second type of boundary effect occurs when the pressure for higher land use densities begins to encroach upon existing suburban communities. For example, a new traffic artery, such as the metropolitan rapid rail system in Washington, D.C., increases the pressure for higher land use densities in suburban communities with access to the system. And, to the dismay of many existing and perhaps longtime residents, these areas often become transitional.

The first of these can be easily illustrated with respect to the San Francisco Bay Area. Davis and Langlois (1963) projected that the sprawling metropolis would cover 7,663 square miles by the year 2000, which would then reach the Sacramento or Stockton urban complex. Given these estimates, Bay Area residents obviously had reason for concern. However, recent estimates by the Association of Bay Area Governments suggest that the projected population will slightly exceed 6 million and cover only 1,069 square miles. Even that constitutes an area with a population density of over 9 persons per acre, including residential, commercial, and industrial uses. By any criteria, it constitutes an urban environment with high residential density, not a suburban environment, extending well beyond some of the existing communities that are attempting to manage growth. For example, even in midsized urban areas that are virtually built-out (that is, they have no room for expansion and relatively little land for development) such as Norfolk and Richmond, Virginia, overall persons per square mile are, respectively, 7.9 and 5.8. Obviously, suburban densities are less.

With estimates as these for growth in the Bay Area, there is little wonder that suburban residents in the path of such growth may have overreacted. Moreover, the same argument may also apply to suburban areas of many large metropolitan areas—it clearly exists in the suburbs of the nation's capital.[5]

Land Use in Medium-Sized Metropolitan Areas

The discussion in the previous section raises an interesting resource allocation question. First, it will be argued that most communities, especially communities in medium-sized metropolitan areas, do not exercise exclusionary land use policies. Second, optimal land use from a societal perspective should focus on land prices. In this context, a medium-sized metropolitan area is defined as one in which there is space for development without creating an inordinate congestion problem. These include most metropolitan areas with populations up to 750,000 or 1 million and perhaps some with larger populations. For cities in this size range, rush hour commuting times are roughly double the travel time during nonrush hours. In general, if the non-rush-hour trip from suburbia to the central city takes 20 minutes, peak-hour commuting time rarely exceeds 45 minutes. The overwhelming majority of these trips are made in automobiles, yet the extended time for rush-hour commuting does not generate a level of frustration or costs significantly high enough to cause a great deal of concern among commuters. Bottlenecks that do occur will eventually be overcome with added infrastructure, but, by and large, the commute justifies the suburban living environment.

There is an interesting political characteristic of the majority of medium-sized metropolitan areas compared with large metropolitan areas. Most medium-sized metropolitan areas do not contain a significant number of communities compared with larger metropolitan areas. For example, in 1975, in the San Francisco Bay Area alone, a survey found nearly 50 communities that were attempting to control the pace of development, and this does not include all communities in the area (Dowall 1982). In contrast, medium-sized cities, especially in the fast-growth areas of the sunbelt, normally contain the central city and relatively few adjacent or outlying county governments (communities). The majority of these communities contain substantial geographic areas of undeveloped land, and, while they do compete for industrial and commercial growth to bolster their tax base, they do not attempt to exclude households by income class. Neighborhoods of all income groups who can afford new or relatively new housing can be found throughout each community. Neighborhood stratification does occur, that is, the average or median family income may differ significantly among neighborhoods within any community. However, suburban zoning among communities does not preserve nor does it attempt to create a homogeneous community population.

The only test of this hypothesis has been conducted for a sample of Pennsylvania suburbs by Janet R. Pack and Howard Pack (1977, 1978), in which they attempted to determine whether communities seemed homogeneous with respect to demographic variables including education, income, household type, occupation, and age. Their findings indicate that suburbs are quite heterogeneous, which runs counter to the exclusionary argument or what one would expect from a Tiebout model. Actually, the Tiebout model could not be expected to work if there are a limited number of communities from which households can choose to locate.

Moreover, suburban communities surrounding medium-sized urban areas, even those with substantial amounts of undeveloped land, do not exclude with respect to the type of housing. Cluster housing developments of town houses and condominiums forming their own neighborhoods or mixed with neighborhoods of single-unit family housing pervade suburban communities of medium-sized metropolitan areas. The increase in cluster housing in suburban communities is thus highly suggestive of the complementarity between land use regulation and the private market for housing. While single-unit family housing once dominated suburban neighborhoods and is still the predominant type of housing, the relative increase in housing prices over the past few years has created a demand for smaller, cluster-type housing. Not only are the housing units smaller than most single-unit family housing, but clustering also reduces infrastructure costs in development. It is also true that the administrative staffs and planning commissions in many communities have taken a leading role, not only in the establishment of ordinances, but in pointing out to developers the virtues of cluster housing. The major issue is, however, that suburban communities have not excluded non-single-unit family housing, nor have they excluded multiunit family rental housing, although they may require lower density levels than exist within central cities.

The major land use conflicts in these communities evolve around maintaining the ambience of the community, recognizing, however, that growth will occur and that the character of the community will change. It is consistent with the notions of Nelson, Rose, and Fischel that society desires to have an input and an impact upon local land use decisions. However, the density, congestion, and ambience problems of suburban communities of medium-sized metropolitan areas are much less severe than in large metropolitan areas. Consequently, the conflicts can be resolved in a way that also produces optimal land use without creating the exclusionary problem or, at least, minimizing exclusion.

Although it would be difficult to demonstrate objectively, the major reason that land use conflicts can be resolved with minimal exclusion is that there is ample space and variety of development within a community to provide a viable location for development in such a manner that the development creates minimal negative spillover effects. The key to this notion is a viable location, that is, a geographic location in which a variety of residential neighborhoods have equal access to the necessities and amenities of a suburban environment. This becomes increasingly difficult in large metropolitan areas since additional expansion normally occurs at the rural boundary. Yet, in large urban areas, the rural boundary may mean an inordinate commute to the central city or the work place for the residents in the outlying areas. The only alternative is significantly higher residential density levels within what formerly have been suburban neighborhoods.

Land Use and the Price of Urban Land

The foregoing discussion thus raises the question of optimal resource allocation in terms of the price of land. Land rent decreases from the central city to the boundary of suburbia and the rural area. Moreover, the larger the metropolitan area, the higher the land rent, in general, in the central city, and the greater the distance to the boundary, the greater the cost of commuting.

Earlier in this chapter, it was demonstrated that land rent is obviously necessary if land is to be put to its best use, but only in this sense is it necessary. Land rent, in itself, is not productive in that each dollar of land rent could be utilized in a productive capacity. This is precisely why land rent has been and will continue to be a controversial issue.

Studies of the rapid growth in California illustrate the impact of land rent on housing costs.

At the core of spiraling housing costs is land cost. In a number of major metropolitan markets, lot cost is more than 40 percent of the cost of the house, as opposed to 15 to 20 percent in recent years. Lot prices in many markets are rising about three times as fast as new house prices. In many major market areas, lot prices have increased 30 percent yearly, with prices escalating more than 50 percent in some cases (Halpin 1980: 279).[6]

Several factors have contributed to this rather phenomenal increase in land prices. They include: the exhaustion of readily available land; antigrowth attitudes creating obstacles to development; lack of infrastructure to support new growth and unwillingness to fund expansion of the infrastructure; increased local and state regulation; environmental regulations that add to costs and delays in development; and speculative buying of land for windfall profits. The list is clearly suggestive of the beliefs of many that growth controls have been the major force behind increasing land values.

Interestingly, however, econometric studies of the impact of growth controls in the same geographic areas suggest that growth controls increased housing costs approximately 6.7 percent. That is, in communities in California that practiced growth controls after 1975 in contrast to a comparison group of communities that did not, it was found that growth controls increased housing prices less than 7 percent between 1975 and 1979.[7] While the significance of the impact of growth controls on housing prices is debatable, that is not the issue here. If land values increased to the extent suggested earlier, it is apparent that they increased throughout the study area, which included communities that did and did not practice growth controls. Otherwise, housing prices in those areas that practiced growth controls would have increased substantially more than 7 percent compared with the control group communities. While 7 percent may not be insignificant with respect to the increase in housing costs, it is apparent that the most important factor contributing to rising land prices is land rent resulting from the derived demand for land, not growth controls.

Moreover, employers in many metropolitan areas are becoming more aware of living costs that affect their profits and competitive position in national and world markets. Areas with high housing costs will experience increasing difficulty in attracting and retaining employers and employees. The beneficiaries of employer relocations will include sunbelt states, satellite communities, and environmentally attractive areas, predominantly nonmetropolitan. What is happening in many California communities illustrates what relatively high land rents can do and is exactly what would be expected in a market economy. Moreover, it is not primarily attributable to land use controls.

For example, there are land rent resource allocative advantages from the location of the Nissan truck plant in Symrna, Tennessee, 15 miles east of Nashville, and the General Motors Saturn plant in Spring Hill, 20 miles south of Nashville. Land rent in these areas approaches that of agricultural land, which is significantly less than the rent of land in or surrounding major metropolitan areas. Whether or not the lower land rent will be reflected in the price of the products, it will clearly be reflected in lower housing prices for employees compared with major metropolitan areas. Even if the employees prefer the residential environment of the medium-sized urban area (Nashville), their land values will be lower and the commute less expensive than in major metropolitan areas.

Land Use and City Size

Perhaps it is time that we entertain the notion of city size from a different perspective. For example, if the San Francisco Bay Area increases to a population of 6 million, land rent, in the aggregate, and the price of housing would significantly exceed that of a more dispersed development.

As economists, we have long held that the growth of large metropolitan areas is attributed to agglomeration economies. This notion begins with economies internal to the firm such as specialization. Economies of scale do not, however, justify large cities. Economies external to the firm, such as linkage effects with suppliers and proximity to the market, and economies external to the industry, such as the availability of a skilled labor market, are necessary. In addition, we have argued that innovation and technological change primarily occur in large cities. All of these are incorporated in what are called economies of agglomeration.

In contemporary society, however, economies external to the industry pervade most regions of the nation and are thus no longer unique to large concentrations of people. Education throughout the nation has reached a level whereby skilled and semiskilled labor markets exist in every major region and practically every subregion of the nation. Moreover, the incredible developments in transportation and communication technology over the past several years have substantially reduced the need for firms to locate in close geographical proximity to take advantage of economies such as quick access to consulting firms. Hence, economies external to the industry exist in medium-sized as well as large metropolitan areas.[8] In addition, technological change probably will not increase as the result of large cities becoming even larger. These developments have unleashed the latent potential for growth in many medium-sized metropolitan areas throughout the nation.

If many agglomeration economies are no longer unique to large metropolitan areas and output per capita is not affected by dispersed productive capacity in advocating any form of land use policy, there are two factors to consider seriously. One is the notion that society desires to have some control over the ambience of the living environment. The other is that aggregate land rent, and therefore housing prices, will be lower which may generate higher real income or may produce a lower nominal wage. Here it has been suggested (although not demonstrated), that both of these might be accomplished in medium-sized cities. Residents have more influence over the living environment with minimal exclusion, and aggregate land rents will be less.

CONCLUSION

Chapter 3 set out an approach to land use that would promote both an efficient and an equitable solution. It began with Henderson's dynamic approach to optimal land use from both the residents' and the landlord-developer's perspectives, an approach that provides excellent insights into land use issues. Yet the approach has received little attention in the literature. Perhaps the previous failure to apply Henderson's model is attributable to rather stringent assumptions, especially the assumption that the landlord-developer owns all of the land within a single community and the number of communities are sufficient to form a competitive market. However, it is demonstrated that these assumptions can be relaxed without violating the theoretical model, and the model can be used to analyze land use issues realistically.

It is apparent that, from the viewpoint of residents of a community, a contract between time period one and time period two is a prerequisite. Residents desire some assurance that the ambience of the community will be maintained. Because the landlord-developer industry is competitive, most developers who enter the market in time period two are only concerned with profits in period two. Therefore, the contract must take the form of a public good; through the local government, residents are able to predict what the community will be like in time period two, as are landlord-developers. Fairness is thus assured by the fact that both parties can predict land uses in the community in time period two. Rose (1984) suggests that fairness results from voice in the process for both residents and landlord-developers combined with the possibility of exit. The developer can always choose not to develop and residents can move, although exit is more difficult for residents. In addition, fairness occurs in the process of continual updating of the comprehensive plan. In practice, it is in this manner that normal land uses are often manifest.

This analysis is obviously consistent with (actually it is almost identical to) the fairness argument presented by Fischel (1985). Both Rose and Fischel argue that fairness can result from being able to predict, but that predictability actually results from the manner in which the community implements land use policy rather than looking at the zoning ordinance or the comprehensive plan. In Fischel's term, it is the "normal behavior" of the community. It is probably true, however, that communities that have implemented managed-growth land use policies have developed comprehensive plans that reflect normal growth behavior patterns. Recall that in both the Petaluma and Ramapo decisions the court was impressed with the thought that had gone into their plan for managing growth. It is highly doubtful that managed growth occurs in communities that have not adopted a plan for growth.

It was argued that planning and zoning were necessary for the efficient allocation of public goods, and, when combined with the free market, efficiency in the use of land would be obtained.

It should be apparent that the approach suggested here will not lead to the outcomes that many might prefer. The single largest investment that the vast majority of Americans have is in their home located in a certain neighborhood within a given community. Because of this, they desire and expect some protection for both. By any criterion, there is a distinction between a suburban community and an urban community. Yet in no way does this imply that exclusion should occur if by exclusion we focus on gross density levels that maintain the ambience of the community. Neither does it imply that a taking should occur.

Communities in the path of urban growth should not be permitted to zone all undeveloped land for large-lot single-unit family housing nor inordinate amounts of land for industrial use. Moreover, most communities do not. Mixed types of housing are found throughout suburban communities, while regulations requiring setbacks, screening, gross density levels by parcel, turn lanes, and many others are often imposed. Piecemeal decision making retains the flexibility necessary for zoning, and occasional deals are not uncommon in communities in the path of urban growth. These do not constitute a taking so long as they are accomplished in a pattern consistent with predictable or normal community behavior.

These arguments, as mentioned, are quite consistent with those of others, especially Fischel—the major difference being that Fischel argues for salable zoning. It is also interesting that so long as the initial entitlements to the density of development are distributed in the manner in which the community has evolved, as Fischel suggests they should be, community growth would occur in the same manner with or without salable zoning. Fischel wants salable zoning to prevent the wealth effect from occurring. That is, he believes communities may be inclined to zone for lower densities than would result if residents had to pay for lower densities.

This approach simply views the land use conflict differently. Communities normally do not make inordinate changes in density levels through regulation. The conflict occurs because landlord-developers request higher-than-normal (with normal being the way in which the community has evolved) levels of density.

It is also interesting to note that higher levels of residential density do not result in significantly lower housing prices, an argument often used by developers. Housing prices will be significantly lower if land values are extremely high. However, in communities where land values do not exceed $20,000 to $40,000 per acre in 1986 dollar value, and this is well beyond the per-acre value in many communities, a density of 20 units per acre will reduce annual housing costs only 2 to 6 percent compared with a density of only six units per acre. While we might quibble over whether a 2–6 percent reduction in annual housing costs is significant, this figure does not include the cost of negative spillovers, especially congestion or additional infrastructure.[9]

In some areas, landlords determine land value solely on the basis of the maximum number of units that can be developed under the existing zoning ordinance. Under this method of setting land prices, increasing the number of units per acre will in no way decrease housing prices through increased density.

Salable zoning is, however, feasible on a small scale such as neighborhoods in transitional stages. These are usually neighborhoods that, in the evolutionary growth of an urban area, are in transition from suburban to urban, that is, basically from a lower to a higher level of density. In these cases, it would be quite feasible for the neighborhood to determine its marginal benefit schedule. Nelson's private market solution, which incorporates salable zoning, would be an excellent way to enhance the flexibility of zoning in these situations.[10]

It is also argued that communities should not be permitted to regulate land for open space or passive recreation nor should they be permitted to regulate in order to protect historical monuments. However, if these are desired by local residents, transfers of development rights provide an excellent, equitable means to a solution.

One important aspect of these suggestions for improving land use is that they can be incorporated into the existing institutional structure with relative ease. A major drawback to any of the proposed alternative forms of land use allocation is the formidable task of implementing a complete overhaul. Realistically, we do not have the luxury of starting afresh. Actually, relatively little is required in the way of an institutional change for implementing land use as proposed here.

Courts at present tend to view the comprehensive plan as a viable means toward managed growth, even though it does not have statutory backing as does zoning. This, in itself, may be sufficient, that is, it may not be necessary to go through the process of providing legal sanction to the plan. The suggestion provided here is that zoning can be viewed as being flexible in the sense that it is piecemeal in nature and that undeveloped land should not be prezoned.

The question remains as to whether communities should be permitted to manage growth in a way that protects the ambience of the community. More specifically, should suburban communities remain suburban or should they become urban? As suggested, perhaps we should begin to view land use from a different perspective. Given the price of land, the cost in negative spillovers that accompanies congestion, and that all agglomeration economies are no longer unique to major metropolitan areas, it is not difficult to understand why per capita real income is now higher in medium-sized cities in the sunbelt states than in major metropolitan areas of many states. Moreover, this has occurred while maintaining the ambience of most communities and neighborhoods.

NOTES

1. There is an unresolved debate in the economic literature concerning the extent to which increases in land values can be taxed away without causing resource misallocation. It could be argued that a percentage of a windfall gain could be taxed away without distorting land use, such as a betterment tax that has been tried in England. For example, a hook-up fee—that is, a lump-sum fee for permission to hook into sewer and water infrastructure—might be neutral with respect to land use. Others have argued that no tax is neutral. For the reader interested in the current status of the debate, see articles in *Urban Studies* from 1973 to 1975 and the *National Tax Journal* from 1975 to 1981. There are others including *Public Finance* in 1978 and *Journal of Political Economy* in 1979.

2. An excellent example of an evolutionary change is the request for a special-use permit to develop a turf farm using the waste from a brewery. While this is a good illustration of recycling from an environmental perspective, there is some chance that the waste may become septic before being absorbed, thereby creating a significant spillover to adjacent neighborhoods. However, if negative spillovers do not result from the recycling process, using the land as a turf farm might be the best use of the parcel. It would

constitute a use that was not predictable, yet it might meet the criteria for optimal land use.

3. For example, Jane Jacobs (1961).

4. For example, Johnson, *Resolving the Housing Crises* (1982), includes three papers devoted to this issue: Bernard Frieden, "The Exclusionary Effect of Growth Controls"; Lloyd J. Mercer and W. Douglas Morgan, "An Estimate of Residential Growth Controls' Impact on House Prices"; and H. E. Frech, "The California Coastal Commissions: Economic Impacts."

There are others, including the works of Schwartz et al. (1979) on Petaluma and the surrounding area. Persuasive studies of the San Francisco area include Katz and Rosen (1980) in addition to those mentioned above.

5. Byron Farwell, "Stay Out of My Loudoun County, Growth Is Not Progress, and Saving an Eden from the Serpents Is Not Evil," *Washington Post,* July 6, 1986, is just one of many articles that have appeared in the *Post* over the past years.

6. Data is not provided to support the percentage increase in land prices. Despite the lack of empirical verification it is apparent that land prices have significantly increased in the growth areas of California. The accuracy of the increases in land rent does not affect the analysis, which is presented in general rather than specific terms.

7. In a recent analysis, Schwartz et al. (1986) suggest that measuring the effects of growth control on housing prices presents severe challenges to researchers. Many of the methods of analysis have theoretical and practical problems that may introduce bias. Their study is an attempt to provide an approach that eliminates, or at least reduces, the bias in several earlier studies. The figure of 6.7 percent was calculated from their data in Table 3 (p. 231).

8. See, for example, Moomaw (1986) and Leven (1985).

9. The logic behind this notion is that simply spreading the lot cost over a larger number of units does not significantly affect annual housing cost, unless the price of land is relatively high. For example, at $20,000 per acre, lot cost per unit is $3,333 for six units compared with $1,000 for 20 units. Assuming $50,000 to be the least cost per unit development, the $2,333 additional land cost per unit reflects a 4.7 percent difference in total cost. This very simple calculation assumes that there are no economies of scale in construction costs at higher density levels. Discussions with local developers suggest that there are few economies of scale in high-density multiunit housing over the construction of three apartments per unit. This simple analysis can be accomplished in a more sophisticated way, but it does not change the results. In major metropolitan areas, the cost advantages are reflected in spreading high land costs over more units.

10. The neighborhood approach to salable zoning has proven successful in several areas. For example, see Robert A. Watts, "After Delays and Deals, Subdivision is Sold," *Washington Post,* January 15, 1987, Weekly Section.

6
Regulating Land Use

In chapter 4 each of the major alternatives to zoning as a means of controlling land use was presented. They included a land consumerism movement, covenants combined with nuisance law and fines, a neighborhood collective property rights approach, the transfer of development rights, a land use intensity system, inclusionary zoning, and a property rights approach in which zoning should be viewed as an entitlement and should be alienable. As a single alternative, each was found to be wanting for various reasons. There are, however, merits of these proposals that deserve serious consideration.

The combination of economic theory and judicial implementation of land use presented in chapter 3 implies that the use of the comprehensive plan and zoning in combination with the free market produces optimal land use. In essence, this implies that the existing institutional structure of land use in the United States obtained through managed growth, that is, through a combination of regulation and the market. In addition, several reasons suggest that many communities will increasingly implement managed growth policies. A major purpose of this chapter is to discuss the implementation of managed growth policies in order to best approach efficiency and equity in land use. However, before proceeding, there is an additional factor in the market for land that has yet to be discussed—a factor that further illustrates the need for regulation in the market for land.

THE SUPPLY OF URBAN LAND

A basic principle of economics is that, given the demand and supply for a good, the market determines the price and quantity, and the solution is efficient. Regulation, therefore, is necessary only when there is some impediment to the market mechanism. A major impediment is that the market for urban land does not conform to normal supply analysis.

The normal characteristic of the supply for a good is that the supply is determined by the costs of production for a given state of technology. In addition, in a competitive market, the costs of production include a normal return to the producer. In the transformation of rural land to urban land, production does take place but not in the same way as commodity production. There are three distinguishing features to the long-run supply of urban land compared with the supply of a normal good.

First, the production of urban land, that is, the transformation of rural land to urban land, often requires additional infrastructure such as sewer and water services and upgrading the transportation system. Infrastructure is provided by the public sector, and it often significantly enhances the value of specific land parcels. Hence, it is provided by public tax revenues, yet it is privately appropriated. Economic theory does not incorporate infrastructure into the supply of urban land. In effect, there is no theoretical supply curve of urban land.

A second distinguishing feature in the supply of urban land is that market forces do not always have the same effect on land transfers as they do in commodity markets. That is, market forces are not always the determining factor in land acquisition and land sale. Several factors contribute to this feature of urban land: the skills, needs, and personal values of farmers often cause them to hold land in the path of urban growth in agricultural use until their retirement; inherited property or land purchased for nonpecuniary reasons interferes with the timing of land sales within the free market; and speculation itself may also affect the supply of land if it becomes an end itself or if land speculators are overly optimistic about development prospects. While many commentators have accused zoning as being responsible for urban sprawl, nonmarket forces in the supply of urban land may be the most important contributing factor to urban sprawl.

An additional unique feature of urban land is the contrast between the short run and long run in the production process. The typical landlord-developer is primarily concerned with his own prospects for profit, yet not completely insensitive to the social values of the community. Some large landlord-developers, especially those involved in large planned unit developments that attempt to attract residents from a large regional market, may be quite sensitive since the success of the development often depends upon community ambience. Nevertheless, a large proportion of the development in most communities is accomplished by landlord-developers whose prospect for profit produces a short-run time horizon compared with the long-run growth of the community. Consequently, from an investment perspective, they do not have an incentive to be concerned about the overall impact of their development on the community. Hence, in many cases, the private sector does not perceive a long-run supply curve of urban land. However, landlord-developers will operate within the framework that exists, although they may oppose long-range land use policies that some consider to be in the general interest of the public.

The combination of these characteristics of the supply of urban land does not permit economists to derive a supply curve for urban land. Lacking a supply curve, in the normal sense, a private market for land will not produce an efficient solution. The combination of the unique characteristics of the supply of land, negative spillovers from noncompatible land uses, and the theoretical argument that demonstrates that residents and landlord-developers need a contract between time periods one and two provide a strong argument for land regulation. The problem is how can we make it work better.

THE OBJECTIVES AND PROBLEMS OF LAND USE REGULATION

The regulation of land use in the community interest involves more than the recognition of spillover effects. This is especially true if, as many commentators have suggested, society is increasingly becoming more concerned about the ambience of the neighborhood and the community. One objective, therefore, is to provide or retain public amenities that would not be privately produced. Another objective is to increase efficiency such as in guiding development and redevelopment of land to more desirable uses and achieving economies of scale in the provision of infrastructure. In addition, there are distributional goals such as making land available to all areas within the community. Perhaps ensuring that the benefits from development are shared by the community as a whole should be added, providing they do not constitute a taking. Accomplishing all of these goals is not easy and may entail a wide range of policies. They should include releasing land from excessive zoning restrictions and permitting the private sector to provide least-cost housing.

The common forms of land use regulation are zoning, subdivision regulations, building regulations, governmental approval, and planning. However, it is only necessary to focus on two: zoning and planning.

ZONING IN PRACTICE

In current practice, zoning poses two difficulties: It does not provide an institutional framework by which social objectives can be met, and it often leads to results that do not conform to optimal land use. Traditional zoning is rigid when, in effect, zoning should be flexible. It makes little sense when rigidly applied to large-scale projects. The newer forms of regulations provide more latitude to builders in their design and have produced greater returns to developers as well as to the community. For example, Planned Unit Developments permit clustering houses and consolidating open space. Substantial areas can be left in open space, more land can be utilized for screening, less land is used for roads, utility infrastructure is more efficient, and less site preparation is required. A better residential neighborhood can, therefore, be produced at lower cost, and community ambience can be enhanced. However, communities often require large tracts of land, sometimes hundreds of acres, before granting the developer a PUD. The concept behind a PUD could just as easily be applied to small parcels of land.

Zoning is a legal instrument, as it should be if it is to be of value to society. However, it has been mentioned several times in preceding chapters that because zoning came before planning, many parcels of land in practically every community are zoned for particular uses that are not consistent with optimal land use. Zoning functions best when it is only one of the means used to regulate land. Regulating land use should begin with a plan for the use of land, and zoning should be used to ensure conformance with the plan.

THE IMPORTANCE OF PLANNING

"Planning has been scorned, mocked, disparaged, and disdained since the earliest days of land use regulation. Worse yet, it has been ignored." These words of Richard Babcock and Charles Siemon (1985: 261) ring of a truth that many who are involved in the land use game do not even understand. These well-known commentators have provided many insights into the problems of land regulation, some of which have come from working in pits as lawyers for the private and public sector. Many of us who have worked in the pit of pits, members of planning commissions and administrative planners, would wholeheartedly agree with their statement.

Babcock and Siemon quote another commentator, Joseph DiMento, who does not believe planning is done well, and, while it could be improved, it does not merit "greater influence":

The planning process is "costly," "conservative," "non-innovative," and "highly subjective." In addition, the actors who plan—not only the professional planners but those who are involved in even the most advanced of participatory schemes—are incompetent to plan. Citizens are ignorant of means-ends relationships and are unwilling to make long-range decisions; when they do take action, results tend to be poor (DiMento 1980: 48).

This broad sweeping generalization of the actions and actors involved at the local level displays an ignorance of what actually goes on in many of the trenches where land use decisions are made. For example, the following describes the personnel of at least one planning commission: a member of the local governing body and a member of the commission who has a law degree and a Ph.D. in political science; a lawyer with a special interest in land use who is a member of a law faculty; a realtor and a developer, both of whom have provided invaluable contributions to ordinance changes that have reduced development costs; a landscape architect; several enlightened citizens of the community who work hard in providing input into the local decision-making process; and an economist, the author of this book. These citizens are not ignorant of means-ends relationships, and they are eager to make long-range decisions.

DiMento further states: "Even planners themselves conclude that implementation of comprehensive plans is an activity that the planning profession has performed poorly" (1980: 49). Many, if not most, of the people involved in the implementation of land use regulation probably agree with the statement. However, the implication of the statement is that it is the fault of those who are involved in the planning process. Perhaps it is true for some communities. However, there are many communities to which the statement does not apply.

The lack of success in the adoption and implementation of comprehensive plans in guiding the growth and development of many communities is the result of the existing process. Zoning came first. As previously stated, the comprehensive plan is not consistent with the way in which many parcels of land are currently zoned and the uses that are allowed in particular zones. This is especially true for the agricultural zones. It is understandable, therefore, that comprehensive planning does not appear to work very well. Growth and development do not have to conform to the plan. Planners, members of planning commissions, and the local governing body can try to manage growth in conformance with a plan, but it is often extremely difficult when the plan itself has no legal backing, and many types of growth legally can occur on land parcels throughout the community that do not conform to the plan.

Despite DiMento's disparaging views of the actions and actors involved in land use decision making, he concludes by defending the following requirement.

Plans that reflect responsible and knowledgeable participation, that are assembled by those who are committed to increasing the predictability and fairness of decisions, that are technically informed, and that balance the interests of all those groups who would be involved deserve to be translated into regulations—official development controls (1980: 147).

Babcock and Siemon further state: "The existence of a plan provides the Court with a yardstick by which to measure the reasonableness and fairness of the particular action taken by the local authority" (1985: 262). In order to be fair to these commentators, the basis of their argument stems from evidence of parochialism by local governments. There *is* credence to their argument.

The problem of parochialism is manifest in what they rightly describe as the NIMBY complex (Not In My Back Yard). They may be right in stating: "The locals are too selfish or . . . close to the actions to bring any objectivity to their judgment" (1985: 262). The statement often reflects the attitude of members of the community who are directly affected by site-specific spillover effects and the attitude of many environmentalists. However, the statement is not an accurate reflection of the decision-making process in general.

Politics in land use decisions can result from the NIMBY complex. Changes in zoning requests that would permit development may be favorably recommended by the planning staff and the planning commission, yet they are occasionally denied by the local governing body through voice in the process. Politics also occasionally enters at the planning commission level. Yet, in most cases, objectivity in the process prevails. Both the planning commission and the local governing body make decisions with a high degree of objectivity.

It may be that many of the commentators who so vehemently oppose the current process of land use decision making base their judgment on a few well-publicized cases in which they have been involved or have learned about from other commentators. They either are not aware of, or conveniently overlook, the hundreds of decisions made annually at the local level, the majority of which are accomplished in an objective way. Nevertheless, the process is not perfect, and it is in need of reform.

What is interesting is that there is agreement to reforming the process, albeit for different reasons. Many critics to the existing process have focused on exclusionary practices including the NIMBY complex. This work has focused on two issues. One, the negative spillover effects from unregulated growth outweigh the inefficiencies and inequities resulting from exclusion with respect to optimal land use. Second, and more important, a model for optimal land use is presented based upon a theoretical economic structure that finds legal justification in administrative law. It is through the model that we find agreement to land use reform suggested by some commentators critical of the existing process. The agreement is in the development and implementation of a plan for local growth and development. Moreover, the notion of developing and implementing a plan for growth has been voiced by eminent land use scholars for many years (for example, Babcock 1966; Clawson 1971; Reps 1964).

It is also interesting, as pointed out in chapter 2, that many communities currently use comprehensive plans in implementing land use policy. The plans may not have legal backing, but they are being used to enforce land use regulation. An inference might be that society will utilize the institutional structure that proves viable.

DEVELOPING A PLAN

No plan will be perfect. It will not satisfy all parties. It should also remain political in nature since the goals of society change with time, and it is through the political process that the goals are manifest. Initially, therefore, the plan should reflect existing goals. In addition, a major purpose of the plan should be to reduce conflicts between landlord-developers and local residents.

The plan itself is nothing more than the comprehensive plan. The comprehensive plan segregates land uses by major category—commercial, industrial, and residential. The plan thus takes into consideration the existing structure of the community, existing infrastructure, and planned infrastructure. Negative spillovers from major land use categories are thus minimized by using natural and man-made boundaries to segregate land uses. One prerequisite is that the geographic area for each major category is adequate to ensure a competitive land market for each category. Communities should not be permitted to designate land for open space or greenbelts within the comprehensive plan. As pointed out in chapter 5, however, there are ways in which open space can be provided equitably. The plan should be relatively rigid within the planning period, although it should be subjected to periodic updates. A distinguishing feature of existing land use policy and the use of the plan in this model is that undeveloped land should not be prezoned. That is, land should not be zoned until landlord-developers are ready to develop.

Planning for residential land use can work well. The existing goals of members of society are increasingly becoming apparent. It is the neighborhood that now seems attractive, because it offers virtues that are threatened by modern society— cohesiveness of moral values, close personal ties, mutual trust, permanence, and safety. There is a declining confidence in the ability of the national and state governments to fulfill this role. Local residents do not desire to leave the future of the neighborhood to the coalition-building in state and federal legislation. They want voice at the local level in the implementation of land use policy.

Basically, suburban residents want a suburban ambience. They do not object to cluster housing, condominiums, and town houses. They do object to residential development with density levels that approach urban densities. When neighborhood safety is threatened and transportation congestion begins to occur, the suburban ambience deteriorates. The negative spillover argument applies to ambience just as it does to site-specific spillovers. Moreover, the same argument applies to urban areas as well as suburban areas. "Cliff Weaver and Richard Babcock have observed that the people who don't believe in urban zoning also don't live in urban neighborhoods. The urban residents who once fled these areas are now rezoning them" (Babcock and Siemon 1985: 264). That is, they are in effect attempting to maintain the ambience of the neighborhood within an urban environment.

In essence, residents desire to maintain the ambience of their neighborhood, and, in suburban communities, residents desire to maintain the ambience of the community. For both neighborhood and community, ambience is reflected in the overall density of development. High net densities within particular parcels of land are not a concern. Suburban gross residential density levels do not preclude multiunitfamily housing, condominiums, town houses, or subsidized housing so long as infrastructure is available and site-specific spillovers are minimized. Exclusion, therefore, does not occur if we focus on site density. That is, if suburban residents have a right to a suburban environment, exclusion does not occur.

Moreover, it is not necessary to establish specific residential density levels or even guidelines. Predictability provided in the contract between two time periods provides the guidelines for residents and landlord-developers. The way in which the community has grown in the past naturally becomes one guideline. The aspect of predictability is the elimination of surprise. Communities should not inordinately reduce density levels, which can be protected through the courts, and landlord-developers should not expect to be able to develop at inordinately high levels of density. Fischel (1985) has suggested the density levels of PUDs might be a guide. Yet this might vary among communities. In the Southeast, the gross residential density of PUDs is roughly two units per acre. While two units per acre, including open space, might be acceptable, PUDs have been developed primarily for middle- and upper-income families. Higher gross density levels would be acceptable providing setbacks are sufficient to protect the suburban ambience. Higher levels should also be acceptable where they do not create traffic congestion.

The plan should be relatively rigid and subjected to continual update. Within the confines of the plan, zoning should be flexible. Moreover, undeveloped land should not be zoned for development prior to development. Thus, all development should be subjected to the decision-making process. Moreover, this can be accomplished without increasing the work of planners and members of planning commissions. Innovative changes can be implemented to reduce the work load and simultaneously speed the administrative process for developers. For example, rigid ordinances could be established to ensure conformance with the plan that would eliminate the need to request a rezoning. Some developers may prefer to meet a rigid set of criteria rather than go through the process of requesting a zoning change, which often includes two public hearings. However, a relatively rigid plan combined with flexible zoning can reduce many of the criticisms of zoning.

First, it will reduce the discretion left to public decision makers. Predictability precludes inordinate changes in residential levels of density. Predictability also includes maintaining community ambience. Here, a conflict often arises between residents and landlord-developers that is difficult to resolve. Many suburban communities do not provide the local transportation infrastructure. It is often provided by the state or a larger municipality. The conflict arises because, in those communities experiencing relatively fast rates of growth, the transportation infrastructure does not keep pace with development. As a consequence, traffic congestion begins to occur prior to the development of many undeveloped land parcels. In order to maintain a suburban ambience, local governing bodies may introduce short-run restrictions that appear inordinate to landlord-developers.

In addition, a relatively rigid plan will reduce delay in the administrative process. Administrative actions that create delays in land development most often occur for two reasons. One, they occur when landlord-developers request zoning changes that are not consistent with the comprehensive plan, realizing that the plan does not carry legal backing. Second, they occur when landlord-developers request inordinate density levels. In both cases, development may be permitted but only after negotiation and changes in the original requests that are viewed by many as a delay in the process. The existence of a relatively rigid comprehensive plan combined with predictability of development will reduce these types of delays. That is, because land use decisions will become more predictable, landlord-developers will be less likely to request development that is not consistent with the plan or development that runs counter to what might normally be expected.

In addition, plans are occasionally presented that are simply ill-conceived. For example, the road design for a subdivision may not be consistent with the terrain of the parcel; the road design, including ingress and egress with the main transportation artery, may create a transportation hazard or the design may not provide adequate safety for fire protection to all residents within the project; or lot sizes may not be consistent with the ordinance. These are just examples of why an ill-conceived plan can create a delay in development. A relatively rigid comprehensive plan will not, however, solve this problem.

Flexible zoning, within the framework of a rigid plan, does retain an important feature of the decision-making process in land use development. The ability to deal or bargain is inherent in the process. It is necessary to the existing process, and it is not unfair to landlord-developers. Planning for growth includes optimal utilization of existing and future infrastructure. Future infrastructure may include land necessary to widen existing transportation systems or add to the existing infrastructure system. Additions to existing infrastructure into undeveloped land clearly enhance the value of private land at public expense. In this sense, private donations of land, private construction of turn lanes, or setbacks from development do not constitute takings. Actually, the ability to deal often works to the benefit of landlord-developers. In the process of bargaining, landlord-developers often obtain a better deal from the zoning of particular parcels than they would receive if the land needed for additional infrastructure is acquired through eminent domain. A proffer to provide larger-than-normal setbacks in order to maintain community ambience combined with higher-than-normal gross density levels is an excellent example.

Planning for commercial and industrial growth is accomplished in the same manner. Because the plan segregates industrial growth to minimize negative spillovers, conflicts between residents or the local governing bodies and industrial development rarely occur. When they do occur, pollution is usually the major concern. Some communities designate an inordinate amount of land relative to the size of the community to industrial use. This should not be permitted, but it is through the courts that enforcement will occur.

In most communities, there will be few conflicts between the community and commercial growth on undeveloped land so long as the plan establishes commercial areas in conformance with existing and planned infrastructure. There are, however, two types of conflicts involving commercial development that arise in many communities. Both conflicts involve areas in transition.

As communities evolve, there is a tendency for commercial development to encroach upon long-established residential neighborhoods. A partial solution to this type of transition is inherent in Nelson's notion of legitimizing private neighborhoods, which includes Fischel's concept of salable zoning. These concepts are discussed in detail in chapter 4. Although legitimizing neighborhood property rights is not permissible or legal in many states, the merits of the idea suggest it should be seriously considered. If legitimizing neighborhood property rights does have merit, state legislatures should act accordingly.

An additional conflict occurs between residents and commercial development in metropolitan areas that have already reached a relatively high level of commercial and residential density. Whether the new commercial development displaces older commercial development or residential housing, the new development usually generates additional traffic. In areas where there is existing traffic congestion, any new commercial development adds to congestion. The adoption of a comprehensive plan will not solve this conflict. Moreover, in some areas it may not be possible to alleviate the congestion. Some land use conflicts probably will always exist.

References

Alonso, William. 1964. *Location and Land Use: Toward a General Theory of Land Rent*. Cambridge, Mass.: Harvard University Press.
Babcock, Richard F. 1966. *The Zoning Game*. Madison: University of Wisconsin Press.
Babcock, Richard F., and Charles L. Siemon. 1985. *The Zoning Game Revisited*. Boston: Oelgeschlager, Gunn, and Hain.
Berger, Peter L. and Richard John Neuhaus. 1977. *To Empower People: The Role of Mediating Structures and Public Policy*. Washington, D.C.: American Enterprise Institute.
Blackstone, William. 1966. *Commentaries on the Laws of England: First English Edition, Oxford, 1765-1769*. 4 vols. Reprint. Dobbs Ferry, N.Y.: Oceana.
Bosselman, Fred, David Callies, and John Banta. 1973. *The Taking Issue*. Washington, D.C.: U.S. Government Printing Office.

Brueckner, Jan. K. 1979. "Spatial Majority Voting Equilibria and the Provision of Public Goods." *Journal of Urban Economics* 6 (July): 338–351.
———. 1982. "A Test for Allocative Efficiency in the Local Public Sector." *Journal of Public Economy* 19 (December): 311–321.
Buchanan, James M., Robert D. Tollison, and Gordon Tullock. 1980. *Toward a Theory of the Rent Seeking Society*. College Station: Texas A&M University Press.
Calabresi, Guido and Douglas A. Melamed. 1972. "Property Rules, Liability Rules, and Inalienability: One View of the Cathedral." *Harvard Law Review* 85 (April): 1089–1128.
Callies, David. 1980. "The Quiet Revolution Revisited." *Journal of the American Planning Association* 46 (April): 135–144.
Clawson, Marion. 1960. "Suburban Development Districts." *Journal of the American Institute of Planners*, February: 69–83.
———. 1971. *Suburban Land Conversion in the United States*. Baltimore: Johns Hopkins University Press.
Colwell, Peter F. and James B. Kan. 1982. "The Economics of Building Codes and Standards," in Johnson 1982.
Crecine, John P., Otto A. Davis, and John E. Jackson. 1967. "Urban Property Markets: Some Empirical Results and their Implications for Municipal Zoning." *Journal of Law and Economics* 10 (October): 79–99.
Crone, Theodore M. 1983. "Elements of an Economic Justification for Municipal Zoning." *Journal of Urban Economics* 14 (March): 168–183.
Davis, Kingsley and Eleanor Langlois. 1963. *Future Demographic Growth of the San Francisco Bay Area*. Berkeley: Institute of Government Studies.
Davis, Otto A. 1963. "Economic Elements in Municipal Zoning Decisions." *Land Economics* 39 (November): 375–86.
DeSalvo, Joseph F. 1974. "Neighborhood Upgrading Effects of Middle Income Housing Projects in New York City." *Journal of Urban Economics* 1 (July): 269–277.
DiMento, Joseph. 1980. *The Consistency Doctrine and the Limits of Planning*. Cambridge, Mass.: Oelgeschlager, Gunn and Hain.
Dowall, David E. 1982. "The Suburban Squeeze: Land-Use Policies in the San Francisco Bay Area." *The Cato Journal* 2 (Winter): 709–733.
Downs, Anthony. 1973. *Opening Up the Suburbs: An Urban Strategy for America*. New Haven, Conn.: Yale University Press.
Dunn, Edgar S. 1954. *The Location of Agricultural Production*. Gainesville: University of Florida Press.
Edelson, Noel M. 1975. "The Developer's Problem." *Journal of Urban Economics* 2 (October): 349–65.
Ellickson, Bryan. 1971. "Jurisdictional Fragmentation and Residential Choice." *American Economic Review Proceedings* 61 (May): 334–339.
Ellickson, Robert C. 1973a. "Alternatives to Zoning: Covenants, Nuisance Rules and Fines as Land Use Controls." *University of Chicago Law Review 40*: 681–781.
———. 1973b. "Suburban Growth Controls: An Economic and Legal Analysis." *Yale Law Journal* 86 (January): 388–511.
———. 1983. "The Irony of 'Inclusionary Zoning.'" *Land Use and Environmental Law Review*. 4: 197–246. Reprinted from *54 Southern California Law Review 1167* (1981).

Fischel, William A. 1978. "A Property Rights Approach to Municipal Zoning." *Land Economics* 54 (February): 64–81.

———. 1985. *The Economics of Zoning Laws: A Property Rights Approach to American Land Use Controls.* Baltimore: Johns Hopkins University Press.

Frech, H. E. III. 1982. "The California Coastal Commission: Economic Impacts," in Johnson 1982.

Frech, H.E. III and Ronald N. Lafferty. 1984. "The Effect of the California Coastal Commission on Housing Prices." *Journal of Urban Economics* 16 (July): 105–123.

Frieden, Bernard J. 1982. "The Exclusionary Effects of Growth Controls," in Johnson 1982.

Grether, David and Peter Mieszkowski. 1974. "The Determinants of Real Estate Values." *Journal of Urban Economics* 1 (April): 127–145.

Guy, Donald C., John L. Hyson, and Stephen R. Ruth. 1985. *Journal of the American Real Estate and Urban Economics Association* 13 (Winter): 378–387.

Hagman, Donald G. 1975. "As a Method of Avoiding the Windfall and Wipeouts Syndrome." In *Transfer of Development Rights*, ed. Jerome G. Ross. New Brunswick, N.J.: Rutgers Center for Urban Research Policy.

Hamilton, Bruce W. 1975a. "Property Taxes and the Tiebout Hypothesis: Some Empirical Evidence." In *Fiscal Zoning and Land Use Controls*, ed. E. S. Mills and W. E. Oates. Lexington, Mass.: Heath-Lexington.

———. 1975b. "Zoning and the Exercise of Monopoly Power." *Journal of Urban Economics* 5 (January): 116–130.

Henderson, J. Vernon. 1977. *Economic Theory and the Cities.* New York: Academic Press.

———. 1980. "Community Development: The Effects of Growth and Uncertainty." *American Economic Review* 70 (December): 894–910.

Hirschman, Albert O. 1971. *Exit, Voice, and Loyalty.* Cambridge, Mass.: Harvard University Press.

Hoover, Edgar M. 1937. *Location Theory and the Shoe and Leather Industries:* Cambridge, Mass.: Harvard University Press.

Hughes, Jonathan. 1983. *American Economic History.* Glenview; Ill.: Scott, Foresman and Company.

Isard, Walter. 1956. *Location and Space Economy.* Cambridge, Mass.: MIT Press.

Jacobs, Jane. 1961. *The Death and Life of Great American Cities.* New York: Vantage Books.

Johnson, M. Bruce. 1982. *Resolving the Housing Crises: Government Policy, Decontrol, and the Public Interest.* Cambridge, Mass.: Ballinger.

Katz, Lawrence and Kenneth Rosen. 1980. "The Effects of Land Use Controls on Housing Prices." Working Paper 80–13, University of California-Berkeley, Center for Real Estate and Urban Economics.

Kmiec, Douglas W. 1983. "Alternatives to the Present Land Use Control System." *Land Use and Environmental Law Review* 14: 279–381. Reprinted from *University of Pennsylvania Law Review:* 28 (1981).

Krueger, Anne O. 1974. "The Political Economy of the Rent Seeking Society." *American Economic Review* 64 (June): 291–303.

Lafferty, Ronald N. and H. E. Frech III. 1978. "Community Environment and the Market

Value of Single Family Homes: The Effect of the Dispersion of Land Uses.'' *Journal of Law and Economics* 21 (October): 381–394.
Leven, Charles L. 1985. "Regional Development Analysis and Policy." *Journal of Regional Science* 25 (November): 569–592.
Li, Mingche M. and H. James Brown. 1980. "Micro-Neighborhood Externalities and Hedonic Housing Prices." *Land Economics* 56 (May): 125–141.
Libecap, Gary D. 1986. "Review of William Fischel's *The Economics of Zoning Laws: A Property Rights Approach to American Land Use Controls.*" *Journal of Economic Literature* 24 (June): 730–732.
Lind, Robert C. 1973. "Spatial Equilibrium, The Theory of Rents, and the Measurement of Benefits from Public Programs." *Quarterly Journal of Economics* 87 (May): 188–207.
Linowes, Robert R. and Don Allensworth. 1973. *The States and Land Use Control.* New York: Praeger.
Lösch, August. 1954. *Economics of Location.* New Haven, Conn.: Yale University Press.
Mandelker, Daniel R. 1976. "The Role of the Local Comprehensive Plan in Land Use Regulation." *Michigan Law Review* 74 (April): 899–973.
Maser, Steven M., William H. Riker, and Richard N. Rosett. 1977. "The Effects of Zoning and Externalities on the Price of Land: An Empirical Analysis of Monroe County, New York." *The Journal of Law and Economics* 20 (April): 111–132.
McChesney, Fred S. 1986. "Review of William Fischel's *The Economics of Zoning Laws: A Property Rights Approach to American Land Use Controls.*" *Southern Economic Journal* 52 (April): 1203–1204.
McGuire, Martin. 1974. "Group Segregation and Optimal Jurisdictions." *Journal of Political Economy* 82 (January/February): 112–32.
Mercer, Lloyd J. 1982. "An Estimate of Residential Growth Controls' Impact on Housing Prices," in Johnson 1982.
Michelman, Frank I. 1967. "Property, Utility, and Fairness: Comments on the Ethical Foundations of Just Compensation Law." *Harvard Law Review* 80 (April): 1165–1258.
Mills, David E. 1979. "Segregation, Rationing and Zoning." *Southern Economic Journal* 45 (April): 1195–1207.
———. 1980. "Transferable Development Rights Markets." *Journal of Urban Economics* 7 (January): 63–74.
Mills, Edwin S. 1972. *Studies in the Structure of the Urban Economy.* Baltimore: Johns Hopkins University Press.
———. 1979. "Economic Analysis of Urban Land-Use Controls." In *Current Issues in Urban Economics,* ed. Peter Mieszkowski and Mahlon Straszheim. Baltimore: Johns Hopkins University Press.
Mills, Edwin S. and Wallace E. Oates. 1975. *Fiscal Zoning and Land Use Controls.* Lexington, Mass.: D.C. Heath.
Moomaw, Ronald C. 1986. "Have Changes in Localization Economics Been Responsible for Declining Productivity Advantages in Large Cities?" *Journal of Regional Science* 26 (February): 19–32.
Munch, Patricia. 1976. "An Economic Analysis of Eminent Domain." *Journal of Political Economy* 84 (June): 473–497.
Muth, Richard F. 1969. *Critics and Housing.* Chicago: University of Chicago Press.
———. 1975. *Urban Economic Problems.* New York: Harper and Row.

Muth, Richard F. and Elliot Wetzler. 1976. "The Effect of Constraints on Housing Costs." *Journal of Urban Economics* 3 (January): 57–67.
National Commission on Neighborhoods. 1979. *People, Building Neighborhoods: Final Report to the President and Congress of the United States.* Washington, D.C.: U.S. Government Printing Office.
Nelson, Robert H. 1977. *Zoning and Property Rights.* Cambridge, Mass.: MIT Press.
———. 1984. "Private Neighborhoods: A New Direction for the Neighborhood Movement." In *Land Reform, American Style,* ed. Charles C. Geisler and Frank J. Popper. Totowa, N.J.: Rowman and Allanheld.
Nourse, Hugh O. 1963. "The Effects of Public Housing on Property Values in St. Louis," *Land Economics* 39 (Nov.) 433–441.
Pack, Howard and Janet R. Pack. 1977. "Metropolitan Fragmentation and Suburban Homegeneity." *Urban Studies* 14 (June): 191–202.
———. 1978. "Metropolitan Fragmentation and Local Public Expenditures." *National Tax Journal* 31 (December): 349–362.
Peterson, George E. 1974a. "The Influence of Zoning Regulations on Land and Housing Prices." Working Paper No. 1207-24. Washington, D.C.: The Urban Institute.
———. 1974b. *Land Prices and Factor Substitution in the Metropolitan Housing Market.* Washington, D.C.: The Urban Institute.
Pilon, Roger. 1982. "Property Rights and a Free Society," in Johnson 1982.
Polinsky, A. Mitchell. 1979. "Controlling Externalities and Protecting Entitlements: Property Right, Liability Rule, and Tax Subsidy Approaches." *Journal of Legal Studies* 8 (January): 1–48.
Popper, Frank J. 1981. *The Politics of Land-Use Reform.* Madison: University of Wisconsin Press.
Reps, John W. 1964. "Requiem for Zoning." *Planning.* Chicago: American Society of Planning Officials.
Rose, Carol M. 1984. "Planning and Dealing: Piecemeal Land Controls as a Problem of Local Legitimacy." *Land Use and Environmental Law Review* 15:241–316. Reprinted from *71 California Law Review:* 837 (1983).
Rose, Jerome G. 1974. "Recent Decisions on Population Growth Control: The Belle Terre, Petaluma and Madison Township Cases." *New Dimensions of Urban Planning,* ed. James W. Hughes. New Brunswick, N.J.: Rutgers University Center for Urban Policy Research.
Roweis, Shoukry T. and Allen J. Scott. 1981. "The Urban Land Question." In *Urbanization and Urban Planning in a Capitalistic Society,* ed. Michael Dear and Allen J. Scott. New York: Methuen.
Rueter, Frederick H. 1973. "Externalities in Urban Property Markets: An Empirical Test of the Zoning Ordinance of Pittsburgh." *The Journal of Law and Economics* 26 (October): 313–350.
Samuels, W. 1971. "Interrelations Between Legal and Economic Processes." *Journal of Law and Economics* 5 (October): 435–50.
Schafer, Robert. 1972. "The Effect on BMIR Housing on Property Values." *Land Economics* 48 (August): 282–286.
Schmid, A. Allan. 1968. *Converting Land From Rural to Urban Uses.* Baltimore: Johns Hopkins Press for Resources for the Future.
Schwartz, Seymour et al. 1979. *The Effects of Growth Management on New Housing*

Prices: Petaluma, California. University of California-Davis, Institute of Governmental Affairs, Environmental Quality Series No. 32.

Schwartz, Seymour I., Peter M. Zorn, and David E. Hansen. 1986. "Research Design Issues and Growth Control Studies." *Land Economics* 62 (August): 223–233.

Siegan, Bernard H. 1972. *Land Use Without Zoning*. Lexington, Mass.: D. C. Heath.

———. 1976. *Other People's Property*. Lexington, Mass.: Lexington Books.

———. 1982. "Property, Economic Liberties, and the Constitution," in Johnson 1982.

Sonstelie, Jon C. and Paul R. Portney. 1978. "Profit Maximizing Communities and the Theory of Local Public Expenditure." *Journal of Urban Economics* 5 (April): 263–277.

Strong, Ann L. 1975. *Private Property and the Public Interest: The Brandywine Experience*. Baltimore: Johns Hopkins Press.

Stull, William J. 1975. "Community Environment, Zoning, and the Market Value of Single Family Homes." *The Journal of Law and Economics* 28 (October): 535–557.

Tarlock, A. Dan. 1975. "Consistency with Adopted Land Use Plans as a Standard of Judicial Review: The Case Against." *Urban Law Annual* 9: 69–109.

Thünen, J. H. von. 1826–63. "Der isolierte Staat in Beziehung auf Landwirthschaft unel Nationalökonomie," 3 vols. Hamburg and Rostock: For a more recent and accessible exposition, see R. T. Ely and G. S. Wehrwein. 1940. *Land Economics*. New York: Macmillan.

Tiebout, Charles M. 1956. "A Pure Theory of Local Public Expenditures." *Journal of Political Economy* 64 (October): 416–424.

Toll, Seymour I. 1969. *Zoned America*. New York: Grossman.

Weber, Alfred. 1928. *The Theory of the Location of Industries*. Chicago: University of Chicago Press.

White, Michelle J. 1975a. "The Effect of Zoning on the Size of Metropolitan Areas." *Journal of Urban Economics* 2 (October): 279–290.

———. 1975b. "Fiscal Zoning in Fragmented Metropolitan Areas." In *Fiscal Zoning and Land Use*, ed. Edwin S. Mills and Wallace Oates. Lexington, Mass.: D.C. Heath.

Wright, Robert R. and Susan Webber. 1978. *Land Use*. St. Paul: West Publishing Company.

Cases

Candlestick Properties, Inc. v. San Francisco Bay Conservation and Development Commission, 11 Cal. App. 3d 557, 89 Cal. Rptr. 897 (1970).
Construction Industry of Sonoma County v. City of Petaluma, 522 F. 2d 897 (9th Cir. 1974), cert. denied 424 U.S. 934 (1976).
County Commissioners of Queen Anne's County v. Miles, 246 Md. 355, 288 A. 2d 450 (1967).
First English Evangelical Lutheran Church of Glendale, Appellant v. County of Los Angeles, California, 55 Law Week 4781 (1987).
Flora Realty and Inv. Co. v. Ladue, 362 Mo. 1025, 245 S.W. 2d 771 (1952).
Golden v. Planning Board of Town of Ramapo, 30 N.Y. 2d 359, 334 N.Y.S. 2d 138, 285 N.E. 2d 291 (1972).
Hills v. Gautreaux, 425 U.S. 284 (1976).

Metropolitan Housing Development Corp. v. Village of Arlington Heights, 558 F. 2d 1283 (7th Cir. 1977), cert. denied U.S. 1025 (1978).
Metropolitan Housing Development Corp. v. Village of Arlington Heights, 469 F. Supp. 836 (N.D. Ill. 1979), add'd. 616 F. 2d 1006 (7th Cir. 1980).
National Land and Inv. Co. v. Kohn, 419 Ps. 504, 215 A. 2d 597 (1965).
Oakwood at Madison, Inc. v. Township of Madison, 72 N.J. 481, 371 A. 2d 1192 (1977).
Pennsylvania Coal Co. v. Mahon, 260 U.S. 393 (1922).
Southern Burlington County NAACP v. Mount Laurel, 336 A. 2d 713 (1975).
Southern Burlington County NAACP v. Mount Laurel, 456 A. 2d 390 (1983).
Village of Arlington Heights v. Metropolitan Housing Development Corp., 429 U.S. 252 (1977).
Village of Belle Terre v. Boraas, 416 U.S. 1 (1974).
Village of Euclid v. Ambler Realty Co., 272 U.S. 365 (1926).
Ybarra v. Town of Los Altos Hills, 503 F. 2d 250 (9th Cir. 1974).

Index

agglomeration economies: declining importance of, 119; defined, 119
ambiance, 30–1, 57–8, 122; community and self definition, 102–3; distinction between suburban and urban environment, 104; of neighborhood and community, 31–4, 130–1; protected by a regulation, 113; and recognition of growth, 31, 107; as related to managed growth, 116–17, 122

Babcock and Siemon, 15; on the comprehensive plan as a yardstick, 129; on criticisms of planning, 128–9; on need for planning, 129; on urban zoning, 131
Bosselman, Callies, and Banta: on the Candlestick Properties decision, 8; Justice Holmes on the general rule for taking, 5; on the myth of the taking issue, 6
building and housing codes, 27

Candlestick Properties case, 7–8
California Coastal Commission, 85
city size: and exclusion, 115–17; and

land value, 115–17; and political jurisdictions, 115–17
coalitions for land use, 64
Coase theorem: applicability to land use, 90; assumptions, 88
collective property rights, 114 (see also property rights)
comprehensive plan, 13, 55: as a contract, 55; description of, 28–35, 131; difficulty of implementation, 129; inordinate changes in, 57–8; and managed growth, 104–5, 121–2; as a means of regulation, 53–55; rigidity of, 54–55; updating, 107; as a yardstick to measure fairness, 129
conflicts in land use (see land use conflicts)
conservation districts, 54–55
courts: current status on land use regulation, 18–20; on managed growth, 7–11; on zoning, 2–3
covenants, 2; as an alternative to zoning, 66–9 (see also Ellickson); criticisms of, 69–71; defined, 67–8; merits of, 66–9

density: and exclusion, 111–12; as related to housing prices, 119
dynamic model for optimal land use, 44–7 (see also Henderson)

economic rent, 14, 21, 46 (see also land rent)
efficiency in land use, 53–4, 103–4, 109; Henderson's criteria, 44–5
Ellickson, Robert, 84, 86, 94; as an alternative to zoning, 66–9; on covenants, 66–7; on normal behavior standard, 94
environmentally critical areas: provision for without regulation, 108–9
exclusion, 48, 110–12; and city size, 115–17; and the courts, 15–20 (see also Mt. Laurel cases); current status of courts, 18–20; and density, 107; and land values, 110–11; and managed growth, 106–7

fairness: in the bargaining process, 51–3, 56, 58–9; comprehensive plan as a yardstick, 129; as a means of predictability, 51–3, 120–1; in mediation, 49–51; as a normal behavior standard, 93–4; as protection from surprise, 51–2; as a reasonable expectation, 93–4; in voice and exit, 51–2, 56–7, 58–9, 108
fair share requirement: in Mt. Laurel cases, 15–16
Federalist, The, No. 10, 48
Fifth Amendment, 4
Fischel, William A., 14, 102, 120; on creation of land rent, 101–2; on entitlement exchanges, 95–6; on fairness, 93, 96–7; on land use regulation as social control, 103–4; on land value, 110; on liability rules and property rules, 89, 95–7; on normal behavior standard, 93–4, 95–7; on PUDs as a guide to density, 94, 132; on property rights approach to land use, 88–96; on reasonable expectation, 93, 95–7; on the taking issue, 92–4; on the wealth effect, 91–2

Henderson, J. Vernon, 38, 56, 58, 102, 104, 119; dynamic theoretical land use model, 44–8; on the need for a contractual arrangement between landlord-developers and residents, 46–7
homeowners association, 73–4
housing prices: affects of subsidized housing on, 43; and growth controls, 117–18; impact of building codes, 27; as related to density, 119; as related to economies of scale, 27
Houston, 69–71

inclusionary zoning, 18; analysis of, 84–7

Kmiec, Douglas: on land rent, 81–3; on land use intensity system, 80–3

land consumerism: analysis of, 64–5; discussion of, 62–4 (see also Popper)
land rent: discussion of, 100–102; Kmiec on, 81–3

land supply: on characteristics of urban land, 126–7; effects of market and nonmarket forces, 126–7; supply curve for, 126–7
land use conflicts: between landlord-developers and local residents, 29–35, 45, 132–4; controversial issues, 30–5, 57–9; mediation of, 34–5, 50–3, 57; noncontroversial issues, 29–30, 58; related to boundary effects, 114–15
land use decision making: administration of, 28–35; piecemeal nature of, 47–8, 51–3, 58, 103, 113
land use intensity system, 80–3
land use reform movement, 24; discussion of, 11–15; at the local level, 14–15; as reflected in landmark court rulings, 6–11; at the state level, 11–13
land use regulation: merits of as a means of social control, 102–7; objectives and problems, 127; on reforming the process, 130 (*see also* zoning)
land value, 115–18, 121; Fischel on, 110

managed growth: to alleviate negative spillovers, 105; court rulings, 9–11; current status of courts, 17–19; and exclusion, 105–7, 116–17; and historical landmarks, 121; and industrial use, 120; and land rent, 102; and large lot zoning, 120; and the need for the public sector, 105–6; and non-exclusionary characteristics, 105–7; and open space, 106–7; and optimal resource allocation, 104–6; and property rights, 112–14; as social control, 102–7
mediation, 33–5, 50
Mills, David, 39–41, 78–9
Mount Laurel cases: Mount Laurel I, 15–18; Mount Laurel II, 17–18; retreat from Mount Laurel I in Madison Township, 17

National Commission on Neighborhoods, 73
National Environmental Policy Act, 24; environmental impact analysis, 24
negative spillovers, 58; empirical evidence, 41–3; regulation to alleviate, 105–6; the theoretical model of, 39–41
neighborhood movement (*see* private neighborhoods)
Nelson, Robert, 14–15, 34: on equity, 74–6; on neighborhood property rights, 72–6, 109, 134; private neighborhoods as an alternative to zoning, 71–5
normal behavior standard: as a means of predictability, 52–3, 96–7, 120–1 (*see also* fairness)
nuisance law: early uses, 2; Ellickson on, 68–70

open spaces: passive, 108; within communities, 107–9; within neighborhoods, 107–9

Pennsylvania Coal v. Mahon, 4–6, 8
Petaluma, 8, 10–11, 97, 120
Planned Unit Development (PUD): description of, 26–7, 34; and open space, 128
planning, 2, 28; developing a plan, 130–3; as a guide to predictability, 132; the importance of, 128–30; and optimal resource allocation, 104–5; political nature of, 130–1; and reducing delays in development, 132–3; regulation and the need for, 105
planning commission, 47–8, 65; functions of, 26
planning staff, 12–13, 47–8, 65–6; administration of duties, 29–35; rising importance in land use decision making, 12–13
Popper, Frank: on land consumerism, 62–66; on land reform movement, 11–13
private neighborhoods: as an alternative to zoning, 71–5 (*see also* Nelson); as a means of social control, 102–4; and property rights, 109–10, 121
proffer, 34, 133
property rights, 11–12, 14; Blackstone on, 14–15, 113; as collective rights, 74 (*see also* homeowners associations); Kmiec on, 80–3; Pilon on, 113; Siegan

on, 112–13; theories of, private and public, 112–14
property rights approach to land use (*see also* Fischel): on entitlements, 90, 92, 95–6; fairness and, 93; on fungibility, 90, 98; liability rule and, 91–2, 97; marginal benefit schedule and, 90–2, 93–4; median voter approach, 92–3, 98–9; normal behavior standard for, 92–5; property rule and, 89; taking issue and, 93–5; wealth effect and, 91–2
property rule: compared to liability rule, 89, 97; defined, 89; as entitlement protection, 95–6
public good: as means of forming a contract, 47

Ramapo, 8–10, 97, 120
rent seeking, 30, 102, 105 (*see also* land rent)
residential private government, 69
Rose, Carol, 103, 120; discussion of quasi-contractual arrangement, 47–53

San Francisco Bay Area, 115
Siegan, Bernard: discussion of Houston, 69–71; on property rights, 14, 112–13

Standard State Enabling Act (SEZA), 25–6

taking issue: and collective property rights, 113–4; discussion of, 4–6; Fischel on, 92–94; and land rent, 102; myth of, 6
transferable development rights (TDR): analysis of, 76–80; applied to environmentally sensitive areas, 108–9; applied to landmark preservation, 77, 108–9; applied to open space, 77, 108–9; the Brandywine experience, 79; discussion of, 76–80; the theoretical argument, 78–80
transitional areas: conflicts generated by growth, 134; enhancing transition, 109–10; neighborhood property rights and, 109–10

zoning: early evolution of, 2–4; need for flexibility of, 55–6, 109–10, 133; and negative spillovers, 25–6; and planning, 2–4, 12, 104–7, 133; in practice, 128; rigidity of traditional zoning, 74, 128; salable, 120–21 (*see also* Fischel and Nelson)

About the Author

MARTIN A. GARRETT, Jr., received his Ph.D. in economics in 1966 from Vanderbilt University. He is currently Professor of Economics at the College of William and Mary and teaches courses in regional and urban analysis. He is presently serving a third term as a member of the James City County Planning Commission. Professor Garrett's publications include articles in *Land Economics* and the *Southern Economic Journal*. He has served as a consultant on several occasions for both local governments and the private sector on land use issues and economic development. His current interests include the impact of rising land prices on housing cost and a history of the economic development of the South.

www.ingramcontent.com/pod-product-compliance
Ingram Content Group UK Ltd.
Pitfield, Milton Keynes, MK11 3LW, UK
UKHW021902220326
469204UK00008B/134